Learning Spaces for Social Justice

Learning Spaces for Social Justice

International perspectives on exemplary practices from preschool to secondary school

Edited by Hanna Ragnarsdóttir and Clea Schmidt

A Trentham Book
Institute of Education Press

First published in 2014 by the Institute of Education Press,
20 Bedford Way, London WC1H 0AL
www.ioe.ac.uk/ioepress

British Library Cataloguing-in-Publication Data:
A catalogue record for this publication is available from the British Library

ISBNs
978-1-85856-518-7 (paperback)
978-1-85856-543-9 (PDF eBook)
978-1-85856-544-6 (ePub eBook)
978-1-85856-545-3 (Kindle eBook)

Typeset by Quadrant Infotech (India) Pvt Ltd
Printed by CPI Group (UK) Ltd, Croydon, CR0 4YY

Cover: Aquarium Graphic Design

Contents

List of figures and tables

Acknowledgements

The Research Centre for Multicultural Studies (http://stofnanir.hi.is/fjolmenning/) at the University of Iceland supported the research projects in Iceland and the publication of this book.

We gratefully acknowledge the contributions of Robert Berman of the University of Iceland, who provided input on this volume, and the staff at Trentham and IOE Press, particularly the editor, Gillian Klein, who supported us in developing our manuscript from the earliest stages through to its publication. We are especially appreciative of the diverse learners, teachers, and school communities who inspired this volume in their efforts to engage meaningfully with issues of social justice. We also express our deep gratitude to the contributing authors and to the schools and parents who supplied cover photographs for this book.

About the authors

Hildur Blöndal holds an MEd specializing in multicultural education and is a doctoral student at the School of Education at the University of Iceland. Her research interests are immigration/migration, mobility, globalization, international education, and diversity in schools.

Annu Brotherus is a lecturer in the Department of Teacher Education at the University of Helsinki, Finland. Following her PhD thesis 'The Activity Culture in Preschool Education from the Child's Perspective' (2004), her research has focused on pre- and primary school education and children's experiences and opinions especially.

Fred Dervin is Professor of Multicultural Education at the University of Helsinki, Finland. He has published extensively on identity, the 'intercultural', and mobility/migration. His latest books include *Politics of Interculturality* (co-edited with Anne Lavanchy and Anahy Gajardo, Newcastle: CSP, 2011) and *Impostures Interculturelles* (Paris: L'Harmattan, 2012).

Thor Ola Engen is Professor of Education at Hedmark University College, Norway, where he is also the academic leader for the master's degree programme in adaptive education. He has conducted and managed several research projects and published extensively in Norwegian and English on questions related to education and cultural diversity.

Antoinette Gagné is Associate Professor of Curriculum, Teaching and Learning at the Ontario Institute for Studies in Education, and Director of the Concurrent Teacher Education Programme at the University of Toronto, Canada. Her interests include diversifying the teaching force, integrating immigrant learners, and infusing issues and strategies related to ESL into teacher education.

Stephanie Soto Gordon is a secondary school ESL teacher in the Toronto District School Board, Canada, and an ESL communication consultant. Her research interests include identity, motivation, second-language education, and teacher education.

Börkur Hansen is a professor in the School of Education at the University of Iceland. He holds a BA in education and psychology from the University of Iceland, and an MEd and PhD from the University of Alberta. His research interests are leadership, school management, school development, and educational governance.

Kaisa Kopisto works as a coordinator for Koulu Kaikkialla (Omnischool), a research and development project funded by the Finnish government. She has been a lecturer and researcher in kindergarten and Early Years education programmes. Her work focuses on day care and pre- and primary education.

Kirsten Lauritsen is a social anthropologist and associate professor at the University College of Nord-Trøndelag (HiNT), Norway. Her main research interests are immigration, refugee studies, and cultural diversity in kindergartens. She has written several books and articles, including the article 'Cultural complexity in Norwegian kindergartens' (published in the periodical *Children & Society*).

Heini Paavola is a lecturer in didactics and multicultural education in the Department of Teacher Education at the University of Helsinki, Finland. Her research focuses on multicultural education in teacher education, schools, and kindergartens. She has 20 years' experience of teaching in mainstream, specialist, and Finnish as a second language classrooms.

Hanna Ragnarsdóttir is Professor of Multicultural Studies in the School of Education at the University of Iceland. She holds an MSc degree in anthropology from the London School of Economics and a PhD in education from the University of Oslo. Her research focuses on immigrant children and families in Iceland, multicultural education, and school reform.

Clea Schmidt is Associate Professor of Teaching English as an Additional Language at the University of Manitoba, Canada. She has formed part of several international consortia focused on diversity in education, and her scholarly interests include advocacy and research related to equity for culturally and linguistically diverse teachers and learners.

Nathalie Sheridan works at the University of Strathclyde, Scotland, managing postgraduate placements, and at Glasgow Caledonian University and the Royal Conservatoire as an academic development tutor. She holds an MPhil from the University of Glasgow and a PhD from the University of Strathclyde. Her research interests include learning, teaching, and marginalized learners.

Geri Smyth is professor and Director of Research in the School of Education at the University of Strathclyde, Scotland. Her research interests focus on the education of bilingual pupils, the diversification of the teaching profession, and the education of refugees. Professor Smyth actively seeks opportunities to co-write with graduate students and her research is predominantly ethnographic.

Foreword

This edited collection is timely and welcome. It adds to a body of literature that addresses educational practice in the context of increasing cultural diversity in many parts of the world. Unprecedented levels of global mobility caused by conflict, natural disasters, and what Stanley calls 'development-induced migration' (Stanley in Goodwin, 2010: 21) have blurred the boundaries that once clearly defined the national, ethnic, and cultural identities of communities – leaving once relatively homogenous nations facing the challenge of coming to know and understand themselves as multiethnic and multicultural. Even countries, such as Australia and Canada, with long histories of multiculturalism are experiencing demographic changes to their already diverse communities. In Australia, for example, recent government policies on refugee and humanitarian resettlement have resulted in an increasing number of refugees, mostly from African nations, settling outside major towns and cities (McDonald *et al.*, 2008) and in areas that have long been predominantly white Anglo-Celtic.

Such worldwide trends have major implications for education systems, for teaching and learning practices, and for teacher education. Evidence from a number of studies suggests that schooling systems are struggling to meet the needs of children whose language, cultural practices, and values are different from those of the dominant majority. In many places in the world, the educational achievement of pupils from certain ethnic and racial groups lags behind that of their mainstream peers (e.g. Gándara and Contreras, 2009; Kamp and Mansouri, 2010; Nakhid, 2011). When they leave school, these pupils are less likely to gain university admission and more likely to be either unemployed or employed in unskilled occupations. In the interest of equity and social justice, we need to move away from viewing these pupils as less academically capable and acknowledge that they are marginalized by mainstream curricula, teaching, and assessment practices that are inappropriate for their learning needs. It therefore becomes imperative to rethink approaches to education that might have been effective in culturally homogenous communities but that do not work for all pupils.

Teachers are generally key to children's educational success. According to Darling-Hammond *et al.* (2001: 10) 'teachers' qualifications, based on measures of knowledge and expertise, education and experience, account for a larger share of the variance in schoolchildren's achievement than any other single factor, including poverty, race and parent education.' 'Of all school variables ... it is teachers who have the greatest effect on student learning outcomes', particularly those from disadvantaged backgrounds (Lingard,

2005: 174). What teachers *do*, and *how* they do it, is closely connected to what they *know*. Teacher knowledge has long been a concern of teacher registration and accreditation bodies, schooling systems, and teacher educators. One salient aspect of teacher knowledge is the knowing of students. This territory is a complex one, however. It is possibly the most important element of teaching since the development of effective student–teacher relationships, and meaningful and relevant curriculum and assessment practices depend on it. It is, in fact, important to everything a teacher does.

Knowing pupils means knowing and building upon what pupils already know, knowing what they still need to know, knowing how they learn best – and knowing them as people. According to Goodwin (2010: 25), to know pupils is to understand the 'informal, cultural, or personal curricula that children embody – the curriculum of home, the curriculum of community/ies, the curriculum of lived experiences.' When teachers know these curricula they understand the nature of pupils' cultural traditions and values – their out-of-school lives – and how these discursive practices shape their learning and responses to schooling (Santoro, 2009). To arrive at this understanding, teachers need to ask the following questions: What cultural knowledge do pupils bring to their learning from contexts outside school, and how can pedagogies acknowledge it as a valuable resource and begin to build on it?

Without such enquiry, teachers may privilege hegemonic curricula and pedagogies and therefore risk failing to engage pupils in meaningful learning. By undervaluing their cultural knowledge, there is a risk that pupils will be seen as deficit and their culture a hindrance to their success. This will continue to position pupils as problems that need to be managed or as subjects that require remediation (Santoro, 2009: 41). In her work on the value of international experiences in increasing preservice teachers' understanding of culture and cultural identities, Dantas (2007: 78) refers to the 'damaging impact of deficit beliefs and stereotypes about what counts as learning ... combined with the invisibility and disconnect of what diverse pupils bring as funds of knowledge in classroom assessment and instructional practices.'

Coming to know culturally and linguistically diverse pupils can be challenging for teachers. It requires them to gain a knowledge of cultures of which they are likely to have had limited experience. It also asks them to question the validity of schooling practices that are embedded within dominant cultural frames of reference – practices most likely seen and understood as normal within hegemonic education discourses. Developing such complex knowledge requires teachers to move beyond their own worldviews to understand those of their pupils.

With pupil demographics changing rapidly – and on an unprecedented scale – the imperative to develop school policies and teaching practices that work for all pupils is becoming increasingly complex. It is almost certain that the classrooms of the future will differ in their ethnic and cultural composition from the classrooms of today; knowing the pupils of today will not be the same as knowing the pupils of tomorrow. As notions of nationhood, belonging, and culture evolve, the challenges facing schools and teachers will likewise continue to have implications both now and in the future for initial and graduate teacher education.

What constitutes effective teaching for culturally and linguistically diverse pupils? What characterizes effective, adaptable, and responsive teachers, and how might initial teacher education best prepare teachers for this increasingly complex work? Such questions never have one answer; there is no one right way of teaching culturally and linguistically diverse pupils, or any pupils for that matter, nor is there a recipe or checklist of actions to follow. What is required is teacher education that produces reflexive and reflective practitioners who have nuanced understandings of what constitutes difference and diversity and who can respond to the concept of diversity as multifaceted and ever-changing. Teachers must know how to 'perform a repertoire of teaching tasks and to choose among them with deliberate attention to pupils' (Ball and Forzani, 2009: 507). They must also understand, as closely connected to the practice, the importance of ongoing reflection, collaborative and individual. By sharing their knowledge, challenging each others' beliefs, and reflecting on their own mistakes, teachers can be encouraged to think deeply about their assumptions regarding pupils, to take risks, to learn from each other, and work together to raise troubling questions about practice. This will be as much for the good of their pupils as for their development as culturally responsive practitioners.

Learning Spaces for Social Justice: International perspectives on exemplary practices from preschool to secondary school brings together eight chapters from Norway, Iceland, Canada, Scotland, and Finland that present examples of good education practice and stress the central importance of teachers to good educational practice. It is heartening to read these success stories at a time when many schooling systems around the world are struggling to address the needs of increasingly diverse pupil groups effectively. The work of the authors who have contributed to this volume gives each of us much from which to draw inspiration in our collective quest to make the world a better place through culturally responsive and socially just education.

Ninetta Santoro
Professor of Education
University of Strathclyde

References

Ball, D.L. and Forzani, F.M. (2009) 'The work of teaching and the challenge for teacher education'. *Journal of Teacher Education*, 60 (5), 497–511.

Dantas, M.L. (2007) 'Building teacher competency to work with diverse learners in the context of international education'. *Teacher Education Quarterly*, 34 (1), 75–94.

Darling-Hammond, L., LaFors, J., and Snyder, J. (2001) 'Educating teachers for California's future'. *Teacher Education Quarterly*, 28 (1), 9–55.

Gándara, P. and Contreras, F. (2009) *The Latino Education Crisis: The consequences of failed social policies.* Cambridge, MA: Harvard University Press.

Goodwin, A.L. (2010) 'Globalization and the preparation of quality teachers: Rethinking knowledge domains for teaching'. *Teaching Education*, 21 (1), 19–32.

Kamp, A. and Mansouri, F. (2010) 'Constructing inclusive education in a neo-liberal context: Promoting inclusion of Arab-Australian students in an Australian context'. *British Educational Research Journal*, 36 (5), 733–44.

Lingard, B. (2005) 'Socially just pedagogies in changing times'. *International Studies in Sociology of Education*, 15 (2), 165–86.

McDonald, B., Gifford, S., Webster, K., Wiseman, J., and Casey, S. (2008) *Refugee Resettlement in Regional and Rural Victoria: Impacts and policy issues.* Melbourne: Refugee Health Research Centre, Latrobe University.

Nakhid, C. (2011) 'Equity for Maori and Pasifika students: The objectives and characteristics of equity committees in a New Zealand university'. *Equity and Excellence in Education*, 44 (4), 532–50.

Santoro, N. (2009) 'Teaching in culturally diverse contexts: What knowledge about "self" and "others" do teachers need?' *Journal of Education for Teaching*, 35 (3), 33–45.

Introduction

Hanna Ragnarsdóttir and Clea Schmidt

As our societies become increasingly diverse in terms of their cultures, languages, and religions, educational institutions face the challenge of providing high-quality education for pupils of diverse backgrounds who bring myriad experiences and knowledge to their educational settings. Similarly, teachers from diverse backgrounds who are educated in a variety of institutions and countries also bring different experiences, views, and contributions to our schools. The principles of equity and social justice in many national and provincial educational policies create yet another task for schools, which must ensure that all pupils have equal access to high-quality education. In recent decades, various models for schooling in diverse societies have been developed with the aim of ensuring that all pupils have equal opportunities for learning.

This book brings together case studies that identify and introduce good practices in implementing social justice in eight pre- to secondary schools in five countries. The implementation varies from one school to another, and each school has had to overcome obstacles in its development towards equity and social justice.

Theories and models of schooling in multicultural and multilingual societies

Many scholars have provided ideological frameworks and models that support school development in diverse societies. One, James Banks (2007), who has written extensively on the characteristics and goals of multicultural education, notes that this development is at least three things: an idea or concept; an educational reform movement attempting to change schools and other educational institutions to enable them to provide pupils, regardless of gender and social class, and from all racial, linguistic, and cultural groups, with equal opportunities for learning; and a process whose goals will never be fully realized.

Inclusive education is a second model, which has increasingly been referred to as suitable for diverse pupil groups, although the notion of inclusion previously related primarily to pupils with disabilities. Inclusion begins with the right of every child to be in mainstream education. It thus assumes that all children are full members of the school community, although possibly with modifications, adaptations, and extensive support (Sapon-Shevin, 2007). Arguing that an adequate definition of inclusion goes far beyond pupils with disabilities, Sapon-Shevin (*ibid.*) looks at the myriad ways in which pupils differ from one another: in race, class, gender, ethnicity, family background, sexual orientation, language, abilities, religion, and so on.

Advocates of multilingual education offer additional perspectives for equity-based approaches to schooling in increasingly diverse contexts. Such approaches tend to be grounded in critical theoretical frameworks that question how and why certain privileged groups dominate at the expense of people from immigrant, minority, and indigenous backgrounds. Models of multilingual education not only question the linguistic discrimination that prevails in many societies; they also suggest alternatives to the normalization of oppressive and exclusionary practices. As Panda and Mohanty (2009: 301), drawing on Panda (2006), elaborate:

> Multilingual education (MLE) is much more than just bringing languages into the process of education; it is, in fact, deeply rooted in a philosophy of critical pedagogy that seeks to actively empower the learners and their communities. If MLE is to be seen as providing a powerful model for the education of indigenous/ tribal and linguistic minority communities, it needs to replace the authoritarian, rigid, preordained knowledge approach of dominant culture-centric education by a system of critical educational experiences, empowering them to become valued, equal, and responsible members of their own and the larger society outside their community and not feel estranged from it.

School reform and leadership

In light of the present changes in the world toward globalism and increasing cultural diversity, Schein (2004) concludes that organizations and their leaders will have to become perpetual learners. This process, according to Schein, requires leaders who have faith in people and who are committed to diversity. In turbulent environments, Schein notes, the more diverse an organization is, the more likely it will be to have the resources for coping with unexpected events. The learning leader should therefore seek to increase diversity and promulgate the assumption that diversity is desirable at both individual and subgroup level.

Diverse and equity-oriented school communities must aim to include staff in development and decision-making processes. Ryan (2006) stresses the importance of looking at leadership as a collective influence process that promotes inclusion. He notes that inclusive leadership is organized to work above all for inclusion, social justice, and democracy, and that it is inclusive in two ways. First, the process itself is inclusive, as it includes as many individuals and groups and as many values and perspectives as possible in decision-making and policymaking activities. Secondly, inclusive leadership promotes inclusive practices.

The book *Schools that Learn* (Senge *et al.*, 2000) is also relevant in this context. In it, Peter Senge and his colleagues argue that schools can be recreated, made vital, and sustainably renewed by taking a learning orientation. According to these authors, this means involving everyone in the system in expressing their aspirations, building their awareness, and developing their capabilities together. In school communities where the experiences and views of pupils and staff differ markedly, active participation in school development is an important part of creating a strong sense of community.

Senge *et al.* (2000: 19) maintain that every organization is a product of how its members think and interact:

> Organizations work the way they work because of the ways that people work. Policies and rules did not create the problems in classrooms or schools today, nor will they eliminate them. The difficulties faced by schools (as in all organizations) are always deeply influenced by the kinds of mental models and relationships at large in the system – at every level, from the teacher and students in a classroom to the national political governing bodies that oversee all schools. If you want to improve a school system, before you change the rules, look first to the ways that people think and interact together. Otherwise, the new policies and organizational structures will simply fade away, and the organization will revert, over time, to the way it was before.

Quoting Sarason (1990), the authors add that the effective reform of schools cannot be achieved until people move beyond superficial conceptions of educational systems and recognize the insidious values and attitudes about power, privilege, and knowledge that keep existing structures, regulations, and authority relationships in place.

Schein (2004) similarly argues that, for diversity to become a resource, an organization's subcultures must be interconnected and must learn to value each other enough to learn something of one anothers' cultures and languages. He concludes that the central task for the learning leader is to ensure good cross-cultural communication and understanding throughout the organization. However, creating diversity does not mean letting diverse parts of the system run on their own, with no coordination. Optimizing diversity, according to Schein, requires high-order coordination mechanisms and mutual cultural understanding.

Developing school cultures that actively build on equity and social justice and celebrate diversity is challenging. Sustaining such changes is even more difficult. Hargreaves and Fink maintain that change in education is 'easy to propose, hard to implement, and extraordinarily difficult to sustain' (2006: 1). Although schools may have developed excellent practices, these are easily forgotten. Hargreaves and Fink hold that 'extraordinary effort and extreme pressure can pull underperforming schools out of the failure zone, but they quickly fall back as soon as the effort is exhausted and the pressure is off' (*ibid.*: 1). Sustainable improvement, according to Hargreaves and Fink, depends on successful leadership, but they also acknowledge that making leadership sustainable is difficult, as charismatic leaders come and go and may take their best people with them to new challenges elsewhere.

According to Hargreaves and Fink (*ibid.*), better-quality education and leadership that will benefit all pupils and endure over time require basic sustainability. They elaborate on seven principles of sustainability in educational change: depth, length, breadth, justice, diversity, resourcefulness, and conservation. In their terms, *depth* means 'leadership for learning and leadership for caring for and among others'. *Length* refers to the 'challenges of leadership succession, of leading across and beyond individual leaders over time'. *Breadth* refers to distributed leadership, depending on the leadership of others. *Justice* denotes doing no harm to and actively improving the environment. *Diversity* refers to promoting harmonious diversity, fostering and learning from diversity in teaching and learning, creating cohesion and networking among its richly varied components. *Resourcefulness* connotes developing and not depleting material and human resources. Finally, *conservation* refers to honouring and learning from the best of the past to create an even better future.

All the schools featured in this book have developed good practices in implementing social justice. While each has faced and overcome obstacles in its development towards equity and social justice, the challenge to sustain their good practices remains. Furthermore, school development does not take place in a vacuum. Every school is part of a community and of society, and each one must act on national and international laws and regulations that are all subject to change. Schools are also subject to international surveys and evaluations that affect their everyday practices and that are closely linked to families and local communities.

Research in ethnically, culturally, and linguistically diverse school communities

In the countries discussed here, demographic changes have initiated debates on various issues related to school development, implementation, and outcomes. These issues include: the processes by which schools have managed to or failed to adapt to increasingly diverse pupil populations; current policies and leadership models in schools and whether these are premised on equity and respect ethnic diversity or exclude, marginalize, and discriminate against ethnic minority pupils and teachers; the extent to which prevalent models of schooling and educational leadership promote individual abilities and cultural capital; and the impact of cultural and religious values on a school's ethos, the relationships between schools and families, and the social and academic experiences of children.

Research in many countries has revealed the marginalization of ethnic minority pupils and teachers in school systems. In North America, the UK, Australia, and Europe, the strengths and abilities of pupils and teachers from non-white, non-dominant language background, as well as their diverse ways of knowing and being, could be acknowledged and affirmed in ways that can inform schooling in these increasingly heterogeneous contexts. Instead, educational policies and practices frequently exclude or devalue these pupils and teachers and position them within a deficit framework. As well as facing overt and covert racism, with the majority language being the standard by which pupil ability is measured, a lack of fluency in the majority language is regarded as deficiency and results in unfavourable labelling and categorization (Goldstein, 2003; Nieto, 2010; Ragnarsdóttir, 2008; Skutnabb-Kangas *et al.*, 2009).

A number of recent studies conducted among ethnic minority and student teachers reveal the former experience of marginalization and barriers to integration within educational settings (see Hvistendahl, 2009; Jönsson and Rubinstein-Reich, 2006; Kulbrandstad, 2009; Lassen, 2010; Paavola and Talib, 2010; Ragnarsdóttir, 2010; Ragnarsdóttir and Blöndal, 2007, 2010; Ringen and Kjørven, 2009; Santoro, 2007; Schmidt, 2010; Talib and Horoya, 2010).

Additional research findings, meanwhile, highlight that while most schoolteachers in many countries belong to the majority culture, their pupils are ethnically and racially diverse. Researchers consider it a challenge that teacher groups are not as ethnically, linguistically, and religiously diverse as their pupil groups (Ladson-Billings, 1994, 2001; Lassen, 2010; Lumby and Coleman, 2007; Ragnarsdóttir and Blöndal, 2007; Schmidt and Block, 2010).

It is also quite common that their leaders belong to the majority culture – in other words, they are white, middle-class, and generally male. The ethnicity, culture, and history of these leaders and the relationship they have with the school community are important factors to consider (Lumby and Coleman, 2007). It has also been claimed that a diverse teaching force makes for a greater understanding of the needs of diverse pupil groups, as it brings a wide range of experiences to the classroom and the school (Ragnarsdóttir, 2010; Schmidt and Block, 2010).

In modern multicultural societies, teachers need to be aware of relevant ideologies, values, and practices for teaching diverse groups of pupils if they are to engage with their increasingly complex profession. Similarly, schools and universities need to acknowledge and respect diversity among their teams of teachers and other personnel.

The schools cited in the chapters of this book have all responded to demographic changes and aimed to implement social justice and develop good practice. The contributing authors are established education researchers who have spent time in schools and classrooms with diverse pupil and teacher populations. Here, we have compiled the results of their work in the form of accessible case studies that illuminate successful practices in diverse schools and make recommendations for further areas of improvement. It is noteworthy that many of the schools and contexts investigated in this volume have not been engaging in these practices in an in-depth way for very long but are only recently responding to issues of diversity. Thus these cases offer insight not only for educators and researchers working in longstanding heterogeneous school environments, but for all those who are just beginning to explore what it means to teach and work across linguistic, cultural, religious, gender, ability, and socioeconomic differences.

References

Banks, J.A. (2007) 'Multicultural education: Characteristics and goals'. In Banks, J.A. and Banks, C.A.M. (eds) *Multicultural Education: Issues and perspectives*, 6th ed. New York: John Wiley and Sons.

Goldstein, T. (2003) *Teaching and Learning in a Multilingual School: Choices, risks, and dilemmas*. Mahwah: Lawrence Erlbaum.

Hargreaves, A. and Fink, D. (2006) *Sustainable Leadership*. San Francisco: Jossey-Bass.

Hvistendahl, R. (2009) 'Å bli kompetent og være til nytte. Utdanning av tospråklige lærere'. ['Being competent and useful. Training of bilingual teachers']. In Hvistendahl, R. (ed.) *Flerspråklighet i skolen* [Multilingualism in School]. Oslo: Universitetsforlaget.

Jönsson, A. and Rubinstein-Reich, L. (2006) 'En yrkesidentitet i förändring? Invandrade lärares möte med den svenska skolan'. *Pedagogisk Forskning i Sverige*, 11 (2), 81–93.

Kulbrandstad, L.A. (2009) 'Introduction: Multilingualism in school and kindergarten'. In Kjørven, O.K., Ringen, B.-K., and Gagné, A. (eds) *Teacher Diversity in Diverse Schools: Challenges and opportunities for teacher education*. Vallset: Oplandske bokforlag.

Ladson-Billings, G. (1994) *The Dreamkeepers: Successful teachers of African American children*. San Francisco: Jossey-Bass.

— (2001) *Crossing Over to Canaan: The journey of new teachers in diverse classrooms*. San Francisco: Jossey-Bass.

Lassen, B.H. (2010) 'Erlendir kennarar í grunnskólum á Íslandi'. In Ragnarsdóttir, H. and Jónsdóttir, E.S. (eds) *Fjölmenning og skólastarf*. Reykjavík: Rannsóknarstofa í fjölmenningarfræðum and Háskólaútgáfan.

Lumby, J. and Coleman, M. (2007) *Leadership and Diversity: Challenging theory and practice in education*. London: Sage.

Nieto, S. (2010) *The Light in Their Eyes*: *Creating multicultural learning communities*, 10th anniversary ed. New York: Teachers College Press.

Paavola, H. and Talib, M. (2010) *Kulttuurinen moninaisuus päiväkodissa ja koulussa* [Cultural Diversity in Schools and Day-care Centres]. Jyväskylä: PS-kustannus.

Panda, M. (2006) 'Mathematics and Tribal Education'. *Economic and Political Weekly*, 61 (2), 14–26.

Panda, M. and Mohanty, A.K. (2009) 'Language matters, so does culture: Beyond the rhetoric of culture in multilingual education'. In Skutnabb-Kangas, T., Phillipson, R., Mohanty, A.K., and Panda, M. (eds) *Social Justice Through Multilingual Education*. Bristol: Multilingual Matters.

Ragnarsdóttir, H. (2008) *Collisions and Continuities: Ten immigrant families and their children in Icelandic society and schools*. Saarbrucken: VDM Verlag Dr. Muller.

— (2010) 'Internationally educated teachers and student teachers in Iceland: Two qualitative studies'. *Canadian Journal of Educational Administration and Policy*, 100. Online. www.umanitoba.ca/publications/cjeap/articles/Ragnarsdottir-iet. html (accessed 11 April 2012).

Ragnarsdóttir, H. and Blöndal, H. (2007) 'Háskólastigið í ljósi hnattvæðingar. Rannsókn á stöðu og reynslu erlendra nemenda við Kennaraháskóla Íslands'. *Uppeldi og menntun*, 16 (2), 161–82.

— (2010) 'Skólamenning og fjölbreyttir starfsmannahópar í leikskólum'. In Ragnarsdóttir, H. and Jónsdóttir, E.S. (eds) *Fjölmenning og skólastarf*. Reykjavík: Rannsóknarstofa í fjölmenningarfræðum and Háskólaútgáfan.

Ringen, B.K. and Kjørven, O.K. (2009) 'The design of a teacher education program for bilingual teachers in Norway'. In Kjørven, O.K., Ringen, B.K., and Gagné, A. (eds) *Teacher Diversity in Diverse Schools: Challenges and opportunities for teacher education*. Vallset: Oplandske bokforlag.

Ryan, J. (2006) *Inclusive Leadership*. San Francisco: Jossey-Bass.

Santoro, N. (2007) '"Outsiders" and "others": "Different" teachers teaching in culturally diverse classrooms'. *Teachers and Teaching: Theory and Practice*, 13, 81–97.

Sapon-Shevin, M. (2007) *Widening the Circle: The power of inclusive classrooms.* Boston: Beacon Press.

Sarason, S.B. (1990) *The Predictable Failure of Educational Reform: Can we change course before it's too late?* San Francisco: Jossey-Bass.

Schein, E.H. (2004) *Organizational Culture and Leadership,* 3rd ed. San Francisco: Jossey-Bass.

Schmidt, C. (2010) 'Systemic discrimination as a barrier for immigrant teachers'. *Diaspora, Indigenous, and Minority Education,* 4 (4), 235–52.

Schmidt, C. and Block, L.A. (2010) 'Without and within: The implications of employment and ethnocultural equity policies for internationally educated teachers'. *Canadian Journal of Educational Administration and Policy,* 100.

Senge, P., Cambron-McCabe, N., Lucas, T., Smith, B., Dutton, J., and Kleiner, A. (2000) *Schools that Learn: A fifth discipline fieldbook for educators, parents, and everyone who cares about education.* New York: Doubleday.

Skutnabb-Kangas, T., Phillipson, R., Mohanty, A.K., and Panda, M. (eds) (2009) *Social Justice through Multilingual Education.* Bristol: Multilingual Matters.

Talib, M.-T. and Horoya, S. (2010) 'Preservice teachers' intercultural competence: Japan and Finland'. In Mattheou, D. (ed.) *Changing Educational Landscapes.* New York: Springer.

Chapter 1

Inclusive practices: Participation and empowerment in a preschool in Iceland

Hanna Ragnarsdóttir and Hildur Blöndal

As societies become increasingly diverse in their languages, cultures, and religions, schools worldwide must adapt accordingly. In Iceland, the legislation governing pre-, compulsory, and upper secondary schools (*Lög um framhaldsskóla* [Upper Secondary School Act] no. 92/2008; *Lög um grunnskóla* [Compulsory School Act] no. 91/2008; *Lög um leikskóla* [Preschool Act] no. 90/2008) is based on principles of equality and stipulates that schools should educate each child effectively. Furthermore, new national curriculum guidelines for the three school levels emphasize equality for all pupils (Mennta- og menningarmálaráðuneytið [Ministry of Education, Science, and Culture], 2012).

This chapter sheds light on the implementation of inclusive educational policies at a preschool in Iceland. The school is innovative in terms of policy and leadership, and actively celebrates diversity while emphasizing equality.

The conceptual and theoretical context

Inclusion and equality in Early Years education

Inclusion in educational settings has been widely researched in recent years and the implementation of inclusive educational policies has been debated. Dialogue on how to develop inclusive practices involving staff and families is increasingly being called for.

Robinson and Jones Díaz claim that dealing with diversity and social justice in the lives of children, their families, and the community is a priority for many Early Years educators. They note that 'the focus on this agenda continues to intensify in a rapidly changing world where the complexities of identities, played out on a global scale, impact severely on local communities throughout the world' (2006: 179). They argue that, to make a significant difference in terms of social justice, educators and educational institutions need to engage more actively, challenging and disrupting the everyday power relations that underpin various forms of inequality. According to Robinson and Jones Díaz (*ibid*.: 176), policies and practices in Early Years settings need to reflect a broad range of contemporary diversity issues and to address the complex issues of diverse children, families, and communities, including areas often perceived by Early Years educators to be irrelevant.

Sapon-Shevin (2007) maintains that inclusion is a model that begins with the right of every child to be in mainstream education. Inclusion thus assumes that all children are full members of the school community, although possibly with modifications, adaptations, and extensive support. Sapon-Shevin argues that inclusion asks teachers to think about all aspects of their classroom – pedagogy, curriculum, and classroom climate – so that they make the environment educative and welcoming for all pupils.

The notion of inclusion has been related mainly to pupils with disabilities but, according to Sapon-Shevin, inclusion goes far beyond such pupils. Inclusion relates to the myriad ways in which pupils differ from one another: in race, class, gender, ethnicity, family background, sexual orientation, language, abilities, religion, and so on. She notes that inclusion as a school policy did not create the differences in our classrooms, but it does allow teachers to name the diversity, value it, and strategize about productive and sensitive responses. The opposite of an inclusive classroom would be 'one that is still (inevitably) heterogeneous, but that makes the differences in the classroom invisible to us and others and asks professionals to teach in some standard way while *pretending* to be responsive' (*ibid*.: 11).

According to Sapon-Shevin, inclusion demands that teachers embrace differences in their classrooms and respond to the whole child and not simply to one aspect or characteristic. Most importantly, teachers must recognize that everyone has multiple identities and that attending to these is essential. Sapon-Shevin notes that being thoughtful and responsive to one issue does not make us less responsive or thoughtful about another.

Promoting positive self-esteem in young children

Early Years educators have a highly important role to play in fostering self-esteem in young children. In discussing equality practices in Early Years education, Siraj-Blatchford and Clarke (2000) argue that identity formation is a complex process that is never completed and stress the importance of highlighting this; to ignore it, they maintain, is to ignore the child's individuality. They note that since an individual's identity is shaped by the effects of gender, class, and other formative categories – which overlap, in often complicated ways – it is important that practitioners are aware of the nature of shifting identities. Each child from an ethnic minority and every girl or disabled child do not perceive themselves in the same way. Siraj-Blatchford and Clarke (*ibid.*: 3) maintain that no group of children – or any individual – should be essentialized, defined, and bound within a definition as if it were impossible for them to escape it. Nor should they be regarded as having an experience that is homogeneous with that of others of their 'type'.

According to Siraj-Blatchford and Clarke, values education aligns with the way that adults and children relate to each other in any setting, and indicates the *ethos,* or character, of that setting. They maintain that, to create a positive ethos for 'equity practices', or fairness, staff in every setting need to explore what the ethos in their setting feels like to the users, such as parents, children, and staff.

Inclusive and democratic practices

Implementing inclusive educational policies in diverse school settings calls for a thorough examination and evaluation of the school context and possible obstacles to equity-oriented practice. Siraj-Blatchford and Clarke (*ibid.*: 14–17) have provided useful criteria for this endeavour, identifying six stages of equity-oriented practice. Stage 1 is the least desirable and indicates the least developed practice.

Stage 1: Discriminatory practice – where diversity according to gender, class, ability, and cultural or racial background is seen as a disadvantage and a problem, and where no effort has been made to explore positive strategies for change. This is a separatist, or overtly racist, sexist, or classist environment.

Stage 2: Inadequate practice – where children's special needs are recognized according to disability but where a deficit model generally exists. If children who perform poorly also happen to be from a minority-ethnic group this is seen as contributory. Gender-based reasons may be given for poor achievement. Alternatively, the children's parents are blamed for being inadequate at parenting.

Stage 3: Well-meaning but poorly informed practice, where staff are keen to meet individual children's needs and are receptive to valuing diversity.

Stage 4: Practice that values diversity generally, and where some attempts are made to provide an anti-discriminatory curriculum and environment.

Stage 5: Practice that values diversity and challenges discrimination, and where equal opportunities are firmly on the agenda.

Stage 6: Practice that challenges inequality and promotes equity, where staff actively try to change the structures and power relations that inhibit equal opportunities.

Similarly, a recent OECD (2010: 216) publication – *Educating Teachers for Diversity: Meeting the challenge* – suggests that, in order to respond to increasingly diverse pupil populations, paradigm shifts from homogeneity to diversity are required. The three stages include:

- Homogeneity, where learners grouped in one kind of educational institution are perceived to be similar and therefore receive equal treatment. Difference is not acknowledged.
- Heterogeneity, where learners are perceived to be different and adjustments are made to come to terms with their different needs. Difference is seen as a challenge to be dealt with.
- Diversity, where learners are perceived to be different and their difference serves as a resource for individual and mutual learning and development. Difference is seen as an asset and opportunity.

Sapon-Shevin (2007) maintains that responding sensitively to differences is at the heart of inclusive teaching. She emphasizes that the children who come to our schools differ from one another – and in many ways. For her, the challenge lies in the many forms that our responses to these differences can take: we can ignore them, we can name them, we can accommodate them, we can celebrate them, we can seek to eliminate them, or we can seek to remediate them. Depending on what particular area of difference we are discussing, our responses may vary significantly, determined as they are by our values, our goals, and our resources.

Equity-oriented and inclusive practices can and should also refer to the inclusion of staff. In ethnically diverse schools where equity is the norm, the inclusive and democratic practice of staff as well as pupils is instrumental. Ryan (2006) stresses the importance of looking at leadership as a collective influence process that promotes inclusion. He notes that such leadership is inclusive in two ways. First, the process itself is inclusive: it includes as many individuals and groups and as many values and perspectives in decision-making and policymaking activities as possible. Second, inclusive leadership promotes inclusive practices. It is organized above all to work for inclusion, social justice, and democracy.

Sustaining exemplary practices is a challenge for schools and school leaders (Hargreaves and Fink, 2006). According to McNaughton (2011), the general challenge of demonstrating sustainability is the requirement to show that when an intervention finishes, the process and programmes that have been put in place are able to continue and will maintain the effects for which they were designed.

The Icelandic background and context

Diversity in schools

Since the mid-1990s, Iceland's population has become increasingly diverse. In recent years, the number of children in pre-primary institutions with a mother tongue other than Icelandic has been higher than in other educational institutions – in 2011 the figure stood at 1,815 (almost 10 per cent) out of a total of 18,961 children. These children had 41 different mother tongues, although their numbers varied greatly between schools (Hagstofa Íslands [Statistics Iceland], 2012).

Official demographics on mother tongues and the ethnicities of teachers in Iceland are not officially registered and therefore not easily available. However, other factors such as gender, education, age, and residence are well documented. Information about staff on the websites of pre- and compulsory schools in Reykjavík suggests that more internationally educated teachers and assistants are working in preschools than in compulsory (elementary and lower secondary) schools (Reykjavíkurborg [City of Reykjavík], 2012a, 2012b).

Equality, inclusion, and democracy – and the obstacles

Legislation governing pre-, compulsory, and upper secondary schools in Iceland is based on principles of equality and stipulates that schools should benefit all pupils and educate each child effectively. However, as current research suggests, many obstacles stand in the way of implementing equality-fostering practices (Bjarnason, 2008, 2010; Ragnarsdóttir, 2008). In the draft policy paper *Shaping the Future: Services for disabled children and adults. 2007–2016* (Félagsmálaráðuneytið [Ministry of Social Affairs], 2006), key goals for policy strategies regarding inclusive practices were put forward. These include ensuring that disabled people in Iceland enjoy the same quality of life and standards of living as other members of society, and that the services, including support staff expertise, available to them are of the highest quality. Considerable emphasis is also put on equal opportunities in education and employment, in both cases possible with the right amount of support tailored to individual needs (Jónasson, 2008). With prejudice or a lack of understanding hindering implementation, such factors need to be combated for this plan to be effective and attainable, given that 'changes in the legislation do not correspond to changes in the conception and/or practices of the actors involved in the process' (Freire and César, 2003: 341).

Although diversity is not specifically addressed in the legislation governing schools in Iceland, as it has been internationally (see OECD, 2010, for example), particular sections of the acts deal with pupils with special needs and those who speak languages other than Icelandic. The OECD (2010) publication *Educating Teachers for Diversity: Meeting the challenge* emphasizes that education systems should ensure that all pupils have equal access to studies and that pupil and teacher diversity should be seen as a resource. Findings from recent research in Iceland indicate that pupils from ethnic minority backgrounds encounter obstacles in educational access and participation (Ragnarsdóttir, 2008), and similarly that teachers from ethnic minority backgrounds experience marginalization and exclusion (Ragnarsdóttir, 2010; Ragnarsdóttir and Blöndal, 2007, 2010).

Method

Research for the case study described in this chapter, where the case is analysed from different angles (Cohen, Manion, and Morrison, 2000), was conducted in 2011 and 2012. The preschool was chosen for its inclusive practices, its emphasis on social justice, and the diversity of its teachers and children. It has also served as a model school for inclusive education.

Data collection included semi-structured interviews with the principal and three focus group interviews with eight ethnic minority teachers: two men and six women from different backgrounds. Each interview lasted between 60 and 90 minutes. The decision to use focus group discussions was based on the views of Morgan (1997) and Flick (2009), who highlight the method's effectiveness in communicating everyday experiences and the way opinions are formed, expressed, and exchanged. The focus group introduced a problem and required its members to use dialogue to solve it as well as they could or come up with an alternative. The method also has a built-in correction mechanism: views that are extreme or not socially shared are weeded out by participants and 'the group becomes a tool for reconstructing individual opinions more appropriately' (*ibid.*: 197).

Yin (2011) claims that group interviews are especially beneficial when the researcher is unsure whether the participants would express their views in the same way in a one-on-one interview. He suggests that being part of a group where views and experiences are shared might give them the confidence to do so. Yin also reminds us that every focus group interview has a certain atmosphere or dynamic that needs to be managed by the researcher, to ensure that all participants can voice their opinions and that none are sidelined by more talkative ones. The data gathered from these interviews were transcribed, coded, and categorized (Flick, 2009; Kvale, 1996).

Targeted observations (Angrosino, 2005), which focused on the daily organization and implementation of inclusive practices, were conducted in two further visits to the preschool. According to Flick (2009), in its various types, observation tries to understand practices, interactions, and events that occur in a specific context, either from the inside as a participant or from the outside as an observer. Flick notes that different starting points are taken in observations to reconstruct a single case: the events in a specific setting; the activities of a specific person; and the particular interactions of several people.

The observations are added to the semi-structured and focus group interviews. According to Flick, observations can change the reality of what is being observed. In our observations, we were aware of this.

Documents analysed included the school policy, a curriculum guide, and an evaluation report from the Ministry of Education, Science, and Culture (Elíasdóttir and Jóhannsdóttir, 2011).

Findings and discussion

Policy and vision

Established in 1975, the preschool was originally developed as a special needs institution with four divisions for children aged 1 to 6. Eight out of 78 places have been allocated annually to children with disabilities and in recent years the preschool has specialized in inclusive education. Following recent changes in its ethnic composition, the preschool is responding to its increased linguistic diversity with a new focus on culturally responsive practices (Gay, 2002, 2010; Nieto, 2010). According to the principal, equality, democracy, and social justice are basic concepts in the policy and, as the main principles in the preschool's vision, they are reflected in its everyday practices. In decision-making activities and development of preschool practices, the principal strives to include the staff, children, and parents, but notes that with a long way still to go she must constantly seek new ways to implement the three basic concepts. The main principles in the preschool's vision are consistent with those identified as exemplary in recent writings on education for social justice and inclusion (Robinson and Jones Díaz, 2006; Sapon-Shevin, 2007; Siraj-Blatchford and Clarke, 2000).

In our observations and interviews we noted a clear connection between the national curriculum for preschools, the school curriculum, and the work that was being carried out. We also observed active participation and involvement from both the children and the staff. During group work the children made choices based on their interests and ability, but were also encouraged and supported to choose subjects that they were initially reluctant to try. The children play an active role in everyday activities at the school, helping out during lunch or snack time as well as assisting a less able friend. The staff encourage them to be independent decision-makers and to be supportive, broadminded members of the school community.

As a testimony to its inclusive nature, parents from other parts of town, including homosexual parents, said that they chose this preschool specifically because of its inclusive practices and ideology; they claim that it teaches their children a valuable lesson about diversity and inclusion – elements that, in their view, are important for active participation in a modern democratic society. They stress that their desire for their children to have the best preparation possible was the reason why they chose this particular school.

A Ministry of Education evaluation report (Elíasdóttir and Jóhannsdóttir, 2011), built on interviews with principals, division heads, teachers, social educators, other staff members, and parents and children, states that the preschool has a clear policy and aims that adhere to the National Curriculum Guidelines and the Municipal Policy for Preschools. Additional statements include the following: the management of the preschool is highly purposeful and loyal to its stated policy; the principal is a strong advocate of the stated policy and works tirelessly to promote equality and social justice; the atmosphere of the preschool is immensely positive; and the preschool shows a clear ambition to implement a policy based on inclusion and equality.

The preschool is a pioneer in the inclusion of disabled and non-disabled children, and also provides consultation for other preschools on inclusive practices. It has received awards for its work in this area. Parents have also confirmed their satisfaction, as the preschool has an active Parents' Association, working in collaboration with staff to develop individualized curricula.

In the Ministry of Education evaluation report (*ibid.*), the strengths of the preschool are stated as follows: it has a clear pedagogical policy; a strong professional leader; well-educated staff who are aware of the school policy and actively participate in its implementation, as well as in varied development work and projects; and good collaboration with parents on pedagogical issues. Its main weaknesses are described as a lack of coherence in the reception and training of new staff and the need for maintaining school buildings.

Having observed active and professional practices and witnessed the policy come to life in different activities and interactions – both between children and staff and among staff members – we can confirm the findings of the evaluation report. Only on a single occasion where we observed the group work of the oldest children did we note some stereotypical affirmations about 'Eskimos' that seemed, in our view, at odds with the school policy. The staff member involved in this incident was young and recently employed; she may not have undertaken adequate training or been exposed to pedagogically relevant practices. This was the only incident we observed that surprised us.

Interviews with staff revealed their fascination with the policy. One of them describes her experience in this way:

> I applied [for a post at the school] particularly because of the policy, I was fascinated by it. I was the first foreign-born person to work in the preschool. I was fascinated by the structure and organization, the pictorial methods ... I had never worked with disabled children before ... The views ... I can see only the positive aspects of it all.

If we recall the six-stage framework described by Siraj-Blatchford and Clarke (2000: 14–17), we are led to conclude that the preschool could be placed at Stage 6 (see above). The preschool's environment is one where inequality is challenged and equity promoted; where staff actively try to change the structures and power relations that inhibit equal opportunities. Any challenges to inequality are also discussed and actions are taken to make the necessary amendments.

In relation to our findings, the activity system model elaborated by Engeström (1987, 1996) is particularly useful as it assists us in examining the dynamic relationship between the individual and his or her community, with a specific focus on the place of work. This was indeed what we saw happening in the participating preschool: a dynamic atmosphere in which all members of the school community were highly valued and their multiple voices were heard. While the whole community shares the same objective, it follows a certain set of rules and divides the labour between capable parties, resulting in a positive outcome.

According to the preschool's curriculum, there are five main aims:

- to work for the equality of all children
- to meet every child's needs
- to work for the cooperation of all professions
- to strengthen the children's social development and work for tolerance and consideration of others
- to strengthen children's general development and thus prepare them for life and the future in a responsible way.

Hence the preschool is organized so that every child's needs can be met. Its policy and work plan also state that the preschool understands equality in a broad sense: human rights are emphasized, and multicultural and equal validity of viewpoints is implemented in every aspect of the preschool.

According to the preschool curriculum, collaboration with parents should be based on respect and trust. To achieve this, various methods are employed to ensure that all parents are reached. For ethnic minority parents, interpreters are present at all meetings and aids such as communication books are used on a daily basis. The Ministry of Education's evaluation report (Elíasdóttir and Jóhannsdóttir, 2011) confirms parents' overall satisfaction with the preschool and states that strong collaboration between the parents, staff, and principal takes place. Parents are particularly satisfied with the individual curricula for each child, which are developed by the partnership and cooperation between the parents and the preschool.

Diverse teachers and children

Compared to others in Iceland, the preschool has an exceptionally diverse staff composition (Ragnarsdóttir and Blöndal, 2010). The group of 35 includes 8 men, 27 women, and 8 teachers from ethnic minority backgrounds from 7 different countries. As well as speaking a wealth of languages, the staff range in age from 25 to 66 and include disabled individuals. Their professional roles include those of sports instructor, pre- and compulsory schoolteachers, and social educators, while many hold a range of university qualifications. But the principal and the teachers regard the staff's diversity as one of the strengths of the preschool.

The Ministry of Education's evaluation report (Elíasdóttir and Jóhannsdóttir, 2011) claims that staff diversity must be regarded as a strength in a preschool that emphasizes inclusive practices. It further states that the equality policy is reflected in many ways, including: the opinions of the staff and parents; the equal rights of all the children; and the comparatively high percentage – 22.3 per cent – of men on the staff.

The findings from the focus group interviews revealed that the staff's diversity was valued by its members and the principal alike. This confirms that diversity is not merely celebrated in this preschool; it is also highly valued.

In many respects, the children in the preschool are a diverse group. In 2011, out of a total of 81 children, the number from a non-Icelandic or mixed background was 27 – or 33 per cent (*ibid.*). Although the preschool provides eight places for children with disabilities, this cohort, according to the principal, comprises more children with special needs, whose disabilities are diagnosed after they have enrolled. Among the children, the total number of mother tongues is 13.

Findings from the focus group interviews and observations reveal the unanimous perception that the children graduate from the preschool with tolerance and a positive attitude towards diversity, both sought-after competences in our increasingly globalized world. Such attributes were credited to the school's diversity and inclusive practices.

Leadership and culture

As stated in the Ministry of Education's evaluation report (Elíasdóttir and Jóhannsdóttir, 2011), the principal possesses strength and a clearly defined vision. She regards the diversity of the children, teachers, and staff as being both a strength of her school and a challenge. The principal's vision is informed by an equality and human rights perspective, and she sees the preschool as a learning community where both staff and children learn from each other. The principal's vision and approach are consistent with views on inclusive leadership expressed by Ryan (2006).

According to the principal, it took certain measures and a degree of effort to change the school's culture and atmosphere from what she defines as a 'women's culture' to one where diversity is openly valued. After some men quit soon after being hired, the principal advocated with greater fervour a school culture in which both men and women were appreciated. According to Sumsion (2005), Early Years education remains one of the most gender-skewed of all occupations, with men accounting for only 1 to 4 per cent of educators in many Western industrialized countries. These statistics have led to numerous arguments for recruiting more men, which highlight the potential benefits for society, for the Early Years profession, and for the children themselves.

The first argument suggests that increasing the proportion of men in Early Years education will disrupt prevailing and limiting assumptions about gender roles and responsibilities and thereby benefit society as a whole. The second focuses on the twin possibilities that a higher male participation rate will enhance the status of both the Early Years profession and those who work within it, and improve workplace dynamics and staff interrelationships. The third argument indicates the advantages to the children themselves, since the presence of more men in Early Years education would provide a greater number of positive male role models.

The principal has now managed to employ eight men, which is quite exceptional for a preschool in Iceland. Her claims that the atmosphere in the preschool has changed following the new additions substantiates the argument posited by Sumsion (*ibid.*) about improved workplace dynamics. The principal's willingness to employ a diverse mix of staff reflects both the strength of her convictions and her desire to achieve her aims of creating a socially just and diverse learning community.

The Ministry of Education's evaluation report (Elíasdóttir and Jóhannsdóttir, 2011) regards the preschool's ethos as very good. It states that the aim of the staff policy is to develop a strong team in which there is effective cooperation between members of all professions. The members of staff interviewed for the Ministry of Education's evaluation report regarded good collaboration, as well as support and praise from others, as among the preschool's strengths.

The staff who were interviewed claim that the preschool's work is firmly based on principles of equity. They say that opportunities for participation and decision-making have been equal, that their voices have been heard, and that they participate actively in the preschool's work and development. They claim to be satisfied with their work environment and cite flexibility, respect, and straightforward cooperation as the factors that contribute to their contentment. One of the staff interviewed noted that the principal is 'very kind and flexible and tries to meet the staff's needs as much as possible'.

The staff describe the principal as being supportive and competent in leading diverse groups of staff and children. They agree that the preschool is a demanding workplace, but highly rewarding nonetheless. One of them says: 'If I can be head of a division in this preschool, I am in a good position. This is a very demanding workplace.' Members of staff also claim that the preschool's policy is thoroughly implemented.

One drawback noted in the Ministry of Education's evaluation report (*ibid.*) was the challenge of educating new staff. The principal has voiced her concerns on this matter and recognizes the need to 'educate' new staff members in the ideological principles of the school. One member of staff highlighted the importance of doing so when she said: 'I have not understood why some of the children here are in a preschool at all.' Referring to severely disabled children, her comments suggest that she has perhaps misunderstood what inclusive school practices are fundamentally about. The school principal is aware of the challenge and is developing measures to tackle it.

Other staff members claim that the preschool's policy and vision are reflected in their everyday work. They highlight the emphasis on equality and equal access and the myriad ways that different aspects of diversity are reflected and accommodated. Referring to the supportive environment, a member of staff from an ethnic minority says: 'I wasn't ready to go to the principal's office and discuss matters with her, but now it is no longer a problem for me.' The staff also describe the personal support they receive from the principal. One member of staff recounts her need to spend long summer holidays in her country of origin and says she has the full support and understanding of the principal in taking longer breaks.

Obstacles and challenges

Despite its strong professional ethos, engaged staff, leadership fuelled by a commitment to its mission, and inclusive pedagogical practices, the preschool is not without its obstacles and challenges. In one of our first visits we were informed about an incident that had caused considerable tension and had led to animosity. It started with a letter from the municipality about the importance of the Icelandic language being part of the curriculum. While the letter was never intended to prevent foreign-born staff from reading to the children, the attendant discussion about language use and accents suggests that the message did not come across clearly enough. Prior to that discussion, a rotation scheme was in place that saw the foreign-born staff read to the children for the equivalent of 15–20 minutes a week. Some Icelandic staff members wanted to make changes to the daily reading sessions so that they only included native Icelandic speakers. This plan was eventually implemented in one of the four divisions – to the extreme dissatisfaction of the foreign-born staff, who saw the gesture as demeaning and discriminative. Confused as to why their limited reading time with the children was suddenly being called into question – given that, from early morning until late afternoon, they were in close contact and communication with the children, exposing them to their so-called 'broken' Icelandic – the foreign-born staff made a strong argument against the new plan.

The effect of this incident was made evident when we spoke to the affected staff members in one of our focus group interviews. As soon as discussion turned to the incident the atmosphere became highly charged. Álvaro, a 45-year-old man from southern Europe who had remained reasonably quiet until this point, spoke with great emotion about how hurt and offended he felt – to the point that he considered quitting his job: 'I read better than I speak.' He could not understand the rationale given, especially since the preschool has specialized language staff to assist those children who need extra support. He also stressed that he and other foreign-born staff acted as valuable role models for children with mother tongues other than Icelandic. Besa, a 53-year-old woman from eastern Europe, echoed Álvaro's feelings, and said that for a while she came to work with a heavy heart. Álvaro said that he felt the incident put the foreign-born staff in a category apart from other staff members: 'We are like second-class citizens, only good enough to set the table and do odd jobs; that does not fit well with the policy of inclusion.' He also questioned what kind of message this would send out to the children, staff, and parents. Other members of the focus group who were not working in the same division did not take this incident and the discussion it generated very seriously. They claimed that it did not affect them.

When we brought up this topic with the principal, she was surprised that it was still a significant issue. She was under the impression that it had been resolved. She had personally spoken to all parties involved and had offered Álvaro the opportunity to move to another division within the school. He declined and is still working in the same division as the colleagues who implemented the initiative. This example also shows the autonomy that the different divisions have, in spite of the high level of cooperation between them, and the school's strong leadership. The principal is confident enough to entrust the heads of divisions with making independent decisions.

In light of this incident one is tempted to ask whether an accent could be considered a social burden or could even be harmful in terms of the teacher–child relationship. Lippi-Green (1997) has documented discrimination against those speaking with an accent, but it has been hard to find credible research data on any harmful effects of non-native speakers on children. Some interesting research has been conducted regarding the 'native speaker myth', especially with regard to English-language teaching. This so-called myth has, according to Rajagopalan (2005), resulted in the marginalization of non-native-speaking teachers as they struggle with feelings of inferiority, and many describe feeling 'second-class'.

We consider Rajagopalan's findings very interesting in relation to the incident over 'who can read to the children'. Interestingly, the person in the preschool who seemed to have been most affected also used the word 'second-class' to express his feelings. Bernat (2008) talks about the power bestowed on the idealization of the native speaker, almost to the point that it clouds our judgement. As Llurda (2009) laments: 'the discussion has typically been based on the overall perception of "native" as positive, in contrast to "non-native" which is perceived as negative.'

Conclusion

The main challenge facing the preschool is retaining the positive ethos that it has already developed. Maintaining its basic values and vision while also supporting active participation and cooperation among its diverse staff members is another challenge (Hargreaves and Fink, 2006; McNaughton, 2011). Even with a high staff retention rate – most have been with the preschool for more than five years – every new staff member brings a fresh challenge. The findings of the study indicate that the responsibility of maintaining the good school ethos rests in many ways with the school principal. She must inform and train each new member of staff to ensure that he or she is capable of being an active and contributing member of the school community. To maintain the basic values and vision within the preschool, the emphasis on inclusion and multicultural education must be reflected through each staff member's actions on the job. This requires that staff understand the preschool's underlying ideology and how this translates into pedagogical practices.

Acknowledgements

This study was funded by the University of Iceland Research Fund.

References

Angrosino, M.V. (2005) 'Recontextualizing observation: Ethnography, pedagogy, and the prospects for a progressive political agenda'. In Denzin, N.K. and Lincoln, Y.S. (eds), *The Sage Handbook of Qualitative Research*, 3rd ed. Thousand Oaks: Sage.

Bernat, E. (2008) 'Towards a pedagogy of empowerment: The case of "impostor syndrome" among pre-service non-native speaker teachers in TESOL'. Online. www.elted.net/issues/volume-11/index.htm (accessed 10 May 2012).

Bjarnason, D. (2008) 'Private troubles or public issues? The social construction of "the disabled baby" in the context of social policy and social and technological changes'. In Gabel, S. and Danforth, S. (eds) *Disability and the Politics of Education*. New York: Peter Lang Publishing.

— (2010) *Social Policy and Social Capital: Parents and exceptionality 1974–2007*. New York: Nova Science Publishers.

Cohen, L., Manion, L., and Morrison, K. (2000) *Research Methods in Education*, 5th ed. London: RoutledgeFalmer.

Engeström, Y. (1987) *Learning by Expanding*. Helsinki: Orienta-konsultit.

— (1996) 'Developmental work research as educational research: Looking ten years back and into the zone of proximal development'. *Nordisk Pedagogik/Journal of Nordic Educational Research*, 16 (5), 131–43.

Elíasdóttir, Á. and Jóhannsdóttir, K.B. (2011) 'Úttekt á leikskólanum Múlaborg 2011: Unnin fyrir mennta- og menningarmálaráðuneytið'. Online. www.menntamalaraduneyti.is/nyrit/nr/6040 (accessed 13 January 2012).

Félagsmálaráðuneytið [Ministry of Social Affairs] (2006) *Mótum framtíð: Þjónusta við fötluð börn og fullorðna. 2007–2016* [Shaping the Future: Services for disabled children and adults. 2007–2016]. Reykjavik: Ministry of Social Affairs.

Flick, U. (2009) *An Introduction to Qualitative Research*, 4th ed. London: Sage.

Freire, S. and César, M. (2003) 'Inclusive ideals/inclusive practices: How far is dream from reality? Five comparative case studies'. *European Journal of Special Needs Education*, 18 (3), 341–54.

Gay, G. (2002) 'Preparing for culturally responsive teaching'. *Journal of Teacher Education*, 53 (2), 106–16.

— (2010) *Culturally Responsive Teaching: Theory, research and practice*, 2nd ed. New York: Teachers College Press.

Hagstofa Íslands [Statistics Iceland] (2012) *Education*. Online. www.statice.is/ Statistics/Education (accessed 11 April 2012).

Hargreaves, A. and Fink, D. (2006) *Sustainable Leadership*. San Francisco: Jossey-Bass.

Jónasson, J.T. (2008) 'Skóli fyrir alla?' In Guttormsson, L. (ed.) *Almenningsfræðsla á Íslandi 1880–2007. Síðara bindi: skóli fyrir alla. 1946–2007* [Public Education in Iceland 1880–2007. Volume 2: schools for all. 1946–2007].Reykjavík: Háskólaútgáfan.

Kvale, S. (1996) *Interviews: An introduction to qualitative research interviewing*. Thousand Oaks: Sage.

Lippi-Green, R. (1997) *English With an Accent*. New York: Routledge.

Llurda, E. (2009) 'The decline and fall of the native speaker'. In Wei, L. and Cook, V. (eds) *Contemporary Applied Linguistics*, Vol. 1: *Language Teaching and Learning*. Oxford: Continuum.

Lög um framhaldsskóla [Upper Secondary School Act] no. 92/2008.

Lög um grunnskóla [Compulsory School Act] no. 91/2008.

Lög um leikskóla [Preschool Act] no. 90/2008.

McNaughton, S. (2011) *Designing Better Schools for Culturally and Linguistically Diverse Children: A science of performance model for research*. New York: Routledge.

Mennta- og menningarmálaráðuneytið [Ministry of Education, Science, and Culture] (2012) *Aðalnámskrá leikskóla 2011* [*The Icelandic National Curriculum Guide for Preschools*]. Reykjavík: Mennta- og menningarmálaráðuneytið.

Morgan, D.L. (1997) *Focus Groups as Qualitative Research*, 2nd ed. Thousand Oaks: Sage.

Nieto, S. (2010) *The Light in Their Eyes: Creating multicultural learning communities*, 10th anniversary ed. New York: Teachers College Press.

OECD, Centre for Educational Research and Innovation (CERI) (2010) *Educating Teachers for Diversity: Meeting the challenge*. Online. www.oecd.org/edu/ ceri/educatingteachersfordiversitymeetingthechallenge.htm (accessed 27 September 2011).

Ragnarsdóttir, H. (2008) *Collisions and Continuities: Ten immigrant families and their children in Icelandic society and schools*. Saarbrücken: VDM Verlag Dr. Müller.

— (2010)' Internationally educated teachers and student teachers in Iceland: Two qualitative studies'. *Canadian Journal of Educational Administration and Policy*, 100. Online. www.umanitoba.ca/publications/cjeap/articles/Ragnarsdottir-iet. html (accessed 11 April 2012).

Ragnarsdóttir, H. and Blöndal, H. (2007) 'Háskólastigið í ljósi hnattvæðingar. Rannsókn á stöðu og reynslu erlendra nemenda við Kennaraháskóla Íslands [University level in light of globalization. A study on the position and experiences of ethnic minority students at the Iceland University of Education]'. *Uppeldi og menntun* [*The Icelandic Journal of Education*], 16 (2), 161–82.

— (2010) 'Skólamenning og fjölbreyttir starfsmannahópar í leikskólum [School culture and diverse teachers in preschools]'. In Ragnarsdóttir, H. and Jónsdóttir, E.S. (eds), *Fjölmenning og skólastarf [Multicultural Issues in Education]*. Reykjavík: Rannsóknastofa í fjölmenningarfræðum and Háskólaútgáfan.

Rajagopalan, K. (2005) 'Non-native speaker teachers of English and their anxieties: Ingredients for an experiment in action research'. *Educational Linguistics*, 5, 283–303.

Reykjavíkurborg [City of Reykjavík] (2012a) 'Preschools in Reykjavík'. Online. www.reykjavik.is/desktopdefault.aspx/tabid-3806/6354_view-2265/ (accessed 13 April 2012).

— (2012b) 'Elementary schools in Reykjavík'. Online. www.reykjavik.is/desktopdefault.aspx/tabid-3809/6353_view-2271/ (accessed 13 April 2012).

Robinson, K.H. and Jones Díaz, C. (2006) *Diversity and Difference in Early Childhood Education: Issues for theory and practice*. Maidenhead: Open University Press.

Ryan, J. (2006) *Inclusive Leadership*. San Francisco: John Wiley.

Sapon-Shevin, M. (2007) *Widening the Circle: The power of inclusive classrooms*. Boston: Beacon Press.

Siraj-Blatchford, I. and Clarke, P. (2000) *Supporting Identity, Diversity and Language in the Early Years*. Buckingham: Open University Press.

Sumsion, J. (2005) 'Male teachers in early childhood education: Issues and case study'. *Early Childhood Research Quarterly*, 20 (1), 109–23.

Yin, R.K. (2011) *Qualitative Research from Start to Finish*. New York: Guilford Press.

Chapter 2

Cultural identity and the kindergarten: A Norwegian case study

Kirsten Lauritsen

Introduction

In Norway, small numbers of children from ethnic minority backgrounds are found in many kindergartens, except for programmes for those in large urban centres. The aim of most of these institutions, however, was originally to provide a good educational programme for Norwegian children – who belong to the country's ethnic majority. This focus still characterizes the content, organization, and composition of staff in most kindergartens. Following changes in the Norwegian population's cultural composition (from 1.5 per cent from an immigrant background in 1970 to 12.2 per cent in 2011), many kindergartens around the country are confronted with an unfamiliar – and complex – landscape, both culturally and linguistically (Statistics Norway, 2011). How these institutions respond to increased cultural diversity will have major consequences for the individual child, for Norwegian society, and for our common future.

The focus of this study is primarily on the professional conduct of two groups of kindergarten staff, and particularly on their exemplary work in terms of social justice and empowerment for diverse learners. It addresses research questions such as: How does the professional practice of the kindergarten influence the daily lives of children as diverse learners? How have professional attitudes towards diversity changed over time so that staff interact with changing diversity in the cultural backgrounds of the children? And how do these changes contribute to what we may call 'exemplary practice' – providing space for social justice and an equality-based participation for all children?

Since the study presented here has been conducted in an area where the kindergarten staff's exposure to cultural diversity is mixed and somewhat limited, it is possible that educators who are more experienced in addressing the needs of culturally and linguistically diverse children will find some of the instances referred to as exemplary practice rather modest. There is, however, a need to study practice in areas with a variety of experiences, including those kindergartens that are only recently confronting cultural and linguistic diversity. There is still a lot to be learnt from the empirical evidence of these kindergartens' responses to those challenges and their anxiety in relation to cultural diversity.

The Norwegian context and current policy

In 2010 the Norwegian government unveiled its policy of offering kindergarten education for all children. As new institutions opened accordingly, 89.3 per cent of all Norwegian children between the ages of 1 and 5 were admitted to kindergarten programmes (Statistics Norway, 2010). As a result there is currently great diversity in kindergartens in terms of the children's age, and of their social, cultural, and linguistic backgrounds. Nationally, children from minority backgrounds accounted for almost 10 per cent of all children in kindergarten, but comprised only 4.3 per cent in the region of our study. Placing fewer children from minority backgrounds in kindergarten does not make the challenges of responding appropriately to diversity easier, however. Teachers working with a single child who speaks a certain language require a particular awareness if they are to foster empowerment and educational development.

The Norwegian government's *Framework Plan for the Content and Tasks of Kindergartens* (Ministry of Education and Research, 2006) emphasizes that identity, language, perspective extension, and recognition are important goals for all children. The fundamental values of kindergartens state that care, upbringing, play, and learning shall promote human dignity, equality, intellectual freedom, tolerance, health, and an appreciation of sustainable development. Kindergartens will promote fundamental values such as a sense of community, care for others, and joint responsibility, and must constitute an environment that supports respect for individuals and the right to be different. Human equality, equality of opportunity, intellectual freedom, and tolerance are important social values that shall provide the foundations for care, upbringing, play, and learning. The ethical instruction provided by kindergartens must take into account the age of the child and his or her cultural, religious, and ideological background. Staff are expected to be identifiable role models, recognize their part in promoting cultures through their own behaviour, and be conscious of their own cultures and values. The

Framework Plan emphasizes that staff must be willing to reflect on their own attitudes and actions (*ibid.*: 20).

Hill kindergarten and Plain kindergarten

The study described in this chapter was carried out in two kindergartens in central Norway – the Hill and the Plain – in 2008–09. The Hill is a municipal kindergarten with 75 children and 18 members of staff, including the principal. Nine places are reserved for children from the local refugee reception centre – which houses 140 asylum-seekers of all ages from around 30 different countries – whose parents are waiting to see if they will be granted residence in Norway. The Plain is a private institution with 54 children in total and 14 staff members.

Both kindergartens are divided into four sections: two for children aged 1 to 3, and two for children aged 3 to 6. Each section has one preschool teacher who holds a bachelor's degree or equivalent qualification, and who is supported by two or three assistants, some of whom work only part-time. In the three to four years of their education, the preschool teacher has studied such areas as education, child development, and child psychology, and undertaken extensive placements in kindergartens under the supervision of an experienced preschool teacher and the university college. However, the majority of staff members in Norwegian kindergartens are assistants. Some of those included in this study have worked in kindergartens for many years but have little or no formal education. The majority of the staff are female, and one of the assistants in each kindergarten is from a linguistic minority background.

A shared focus among all kindergartens in Norway – including the two in this study – is on language skills. Outdoor activities are also important, and there are regular trips to different areas of the country. A couple of years before the study was undertaken, both institutions participated in a project in which one or two staff members attended classes at a local university college. There they undertook professional development in relation to working in a culturally diverse kindergarten and covered subjects such as language training for multilingual children and communication with parents and children across different languages, religions, and traditions. For a limited period of time both kindergartens ran their own development projects that focused on bilingualism and cooperation between minority parents and the kindergartens. Together with three other kindergartens, they formed a network that received mentoring from the university college prior to the commencement of the project. To a certain extent, then, the staff were familiar with issues of cultural diversity. The classes that they attended were part of a limited, short-term, nationally initiated development project with experienced researchers and practitioners as presenters, though the classes conferred no university credits.

Theoretical approaches and methodology

The Norwegian anthropologist Marianne Gullestad has shifted the focus in Norwegian research on diversity from the study of 'immigrant groups' to an investigation of 'Norwegian-ness'. She also looks at relations between individuals or groups in a culturally complex society (Gullestad, 1996, 2002, 2006). Gullestad sees people's representations of the world as their interpretations of it, and therefore as constructions, some of which are presented as 'natural' and potentially hegemonic (Gullestad, 2002). In this chapter, diversity is understood in a wide sense, as constructed through discursive practices in the kindergarten. In a study of diversity in schools in Oslo, An-Magritt Hauge presents the schools as being on a continuum between two ideal types: 'resource-oriented' and 'problem-oriented' (Hauge, 2007). While neither of the kindergartens in this study is solely problem- or resource-oriented, this distinction might determine whether the staff's ways of thinking and acting made the environment 'Norwegian/monocultural' or 'international' – where a cultural difference is seen as just one of many differences.

In a monocultural-oriented kindergarten, children from ethnic minorities are seen to create problems and challenges that are different from what its staff are used to. The kindergarten focuses on what is (visibly) different, assuming that the majority-dominant culture should characterize their work. An alternative to this approach is to accept that all children are different – and it is the kindergarten's job to welcome this diversity and its effects on the staff's daily work. Whether or not this approach is taken determines whether children from culturally diverse backgrounds are perceived as 'difficult and demanding' or as a self-evident and integral part of the kindergarten (Staunæs, 2004).

Creating an equality-based environment for all children in a kindergarten raises questions of identity and belonging. These questions have long been central to the social sciences (Barth, 1969; Cummins, 1996; Hall, 1996; Migdal, 2004). In this chapter, identity refers to processes in which children are divided into groups, separated by border markers that define who belongs where. The American professor of international studies, Joel Migdal, uses the term 'boundaries' to refer to the point at which 'the way things are done changes, at which "we" and "they" begin, at which certain rules for behaviour no longer obtain and others take hold' (Migdal,

2004). Boundaries between people are created by processes in which certain actions are taken, and in which those actions are rejected or counteracted. According to Migdal, boundaries have two functions: as virtual checkpoints and as mental maps. Migdal's understanding of boundaries alerts us to those distinctions that might be used to establish group membership in a kindergarten and to make a distinction between those who are included in a group and those who are not.

Data collection for this chapter saw the researcher observe participants for two two-week periods. It also included interviews with principals, preschool teachers, and assistants; an analysis of written reports and internet material; and observations of meetings between staff members.[1] The study took place in 2008 and 2009 and explored the following areas: the kindergartens' experiences, negotiations, and processes of change; how – and whether – they adapted to new challenges; and whether there was any resistance to change among the staff. In the following sections some examples are presented to illustrate how the kindergartens progressed towards a more inclusive practice for both minority and majority children.[2] This practice was mentioned recurrently in several interviews with the staff, and seemed to underpin the changes in their interaction with parents and children from minority backgrounds.

From 'general scepticism' to 'real problems'

Several interviews with staff members distinguished the time 'before' they started to receive children from the reception centre from 'now', when they felt more confident in addressing cultural and linguistic diversity. Their stories highlight a positive trajectory as the staff, children, and majority-ethnic parents replaced their scepticism and resistance with an everyday, practical approach.

Prior to this shift in attitude, interviews suggested that several employees at the kindergarten were initially very sceptical about receiving children from the reception centre. One of the preschool teachers said: 'When we first heard that we were going to do it, many people were against it and didn't want to ....' Having previously received children from refugee backgrounds, the staff assumed that parents from the reception centre lacked knowledge about how a Norwegian kindergarten works. Apprehensions concerned possible conflicts about 'being on time' when delivering and picking up a child, about smaller children sleeping in their prams outdoors, and about Christmas celebrations, visiting the local church, and other religious matters. This scepticism extended to further assumptions about language problems, concerns that the parents would not understand 'Norwegian culture', and, finally, that staff might be exposed to diseases.

The staff also felt that preparing to receive the minority children added to their already stressful workload. They distinguished between working with majority-ethnic children – which was part of their 'normal' work life – and working with 'ethnic minority' children, which was seen, by contrast, as 'difficult and demanding', as Staunæs (2004) put it – not as a self-evident and integral part of their work. Not all staff reacted with scepticism, however. One enlightened employee said she was convinced that personally knowing someone from a minority background was crucial to her having a respectful attitude. She held the media largely responsible for the negative images that the employees had. For her, knowing just one foreign person was enough to change her preconceptions.

As well as from the teachers, there was also some initial scepticism among the parents and children from the majority background, as one preschool teacher expresses: 'The "dark" children were frequently blamed for whatever was wrong … first of all by the parents, because they had children themselves that weren't easy, and it was convenient to blame someone else.' This quotation comes from one of the staff members who had been open to receiving children from the reception centre, and had played an active part in preparing her department for the task. I have interpreted her reference to skin colour ('dark') as an attempt to avoid using concepts referring to race, but to still use a term that is not accepted in antiracist literature (Fanon, 1986; Hall, 1996). My interpretation corroborates her narrative, in which she talks about how insecure she and the rest of the staff were – and maybe to a certain extent still are – about using terms that are loaded and unacceptable when referring to race relations and skin colour. The woman went on to recount how this scepticism among the staff and parents was countered by a series of information meetings where doctors and refugee consultants were invited to share their knowledge and experiences. The staff reported that the meetings helped them develop their understanding of 'other cultures', and allowed them to see that people do not make the decision to flee their country easily, or to bring their children with them to a foreign country.

Separate meetings were held among the staff to discuss the challenges that they presumed they would face and to reflect on possible solutions. At these meetings the staff initially described a worst-case scenario and highlighted the so-called differences – or, in Migdal's terms, borders – and potential problems between 'us' (staff, parents, and children from the majority-ethnic background), and 'them' (parents and children from a minority background). Looking back on those meetings, one member of staff suggested that bringing this negativity out into the open was the first step in the process of staff changing these attitudes. As that process continued, staff with previous experience of working with children from minority backgrounds, or who had mastered English or another second language, provided important practical assistance, knowledge, and advice. Such skills and qualifications are not the preserve of formally educated staff; they may just as easily be found in an assistant or a kitchen worker.

The staff's daily encounters with minority parents and children eventually allowed them to challenge or even change their initial preconceptions. One experience that the staff reported on concerned the parents of two children who belonged to two different ethnic groups. Although the groups were still at war in their country, both parents seemed to get along fine when they delivered or collected their children. Another case involved a Somali single mother with two small girls. This woman was often emotional and had clearly had a difficult time. She was sometimes given a cup of tea and invited to lie down on a sofa in the kindergarten for a while. The staff found it difficult to handle: 'How do we cope with things like that? We just let her lie there without doing anything much, talked a little, and gave her a cup of tea….' Over time, getting to know specific individuals from refugee backgrounds broadened the staff's horizons, allowing them to see not just differences between people, but how minority parents' lives, grievances, and frustrations compared with their own. This, in turn, developed their empathy and understanding. The fieldwork interviews and observations confirmed the staff's conviction that all staff, as well as children and their parents, should experience cultural diversity, irrespective of their background.

Initial incidents involving the children suggested that skin colour served as a marker of difference. One of the preschool teachers said: 'I experienced an episode where a child didn't want to hold hands with anyone dark; he obviously felt it was disgusting.' The quotation highlights the association between 'dark' and 'disgusting', in contrast to Norwegian kids, who are seen as 'light' or 'clean'. The tendency to categorize children on the basis of such notions is well known; Mary Douglas, for example, provides a classic analysis of it in her famous book *Purity and Danger* (Douglas, 2002). In this incident the Norwegian children appear to use skin colour as a marker of difference, something to navigate by. As one of Migdal's border markers, it is the means by which children are divided into different categories. Categorizing children according to this particular feature – skin colour – represents a ranking – with the majority-ethnic kids coming out on top because they are light, not dark, and not 'disgusting' to hold hands with.

The staff were very concerned about that incident and took immediate action. They tried to focus on friendship – something that all the children could associate themselves with – and, by making it a theme for a longer period, sought to emphasize the importance of being of equal value, regardless of appearance or abilities. The staff's efforts paid off, as there were scarcely any similar incidents in the years that followed. The staff continued to remain alert to problems of this kind, however, and tried to stimulate play and activities that transcended linguistic or cultural differences. Informants confirmed that references to skin colour seemed to have vanished from daily encounters among staff, parents, and children. These changes happened despite the staff's initial scepticism. The staff's perceived difficulties in dealing with minority parents and children diminished partly as a consequence of their day-to-day interaction with them.

Such changes elicit unanswered questions: do they indicate a genuine acceptance of difference, or were they the result of staff suppressing their feelings following the aforementioned incident? Might the change in practice have influenced the staff's way of thinking? Whatever the reason, the incident marked a turning point – what Migdal terms a 'border marker' – in the staff's practice. One preschool teacher says: '[now] whether we get a new child from the asylum centre or it is a new Norwegian kid, it's not a big difference to the staff....' They still have disagreements and difficulties when communicating, just as they do with all children and parents – but as one preschool teacher said: 'These are real problems and not anxiety about something we don't know....'

From areas of tension to practical solutions

When the staff first encountered the kindergarten's increased cultural diversity, their border markers seemed to relate to particular areas of its daily life. Faced with situations they had no previous experience of, the staff used border markers to deal with the dilemmas and tensions that increasingly resulted. One area of tension concerned food. In their first conversation with parents, staff at the kindergarten asked whether there were any foods that their child should not eat – Muslims typically do not eat pork, for example. Information relayed in these conversations was shared with members of the department that the child joined and alternatives were provided whenever meals containing meat, for example, were served. The staff were very mindful about following parents' instructions about food, just as they were about any other prohibitions concerning religious or cultural traditions. However, they also spoke about their early tendency to generalize; they automatically assumed that, if the parents were Muslims, the child should not eat pork. At one kindergarten, for example, which had eight Muslim children at the time, staff found that only one child's parents had instructed them to observe this prohibition. Through talks and discussions, they moved from the assumption that 'Muslims don't eat pork' to 'some Muslims don't eat pork' (Lauritsen, 2011).

The staff had also been upset by what the minority children brought for lunch: 'Their lunches can be very exotic sometimes. Sausage with bread, meat, rarely slices of brown bread.' Their frustration soon diminished, however, as they spent more time with the children and increased their experience and cultural competence. They came to see such details as being of little importance, so long as the lunches were generally healthy. What began as a border marker between 'us' and 'them' soon became nothing more than a practical issue. These changes were also reflected in other areas as the staff replaced their generalizations with an approach that took individual considerations into account.

Another area of tension was clothing. Although the staff expected it to be difficult for people from warmer climates to adjust to Norwegian temperatures, it was difficult for them to inform parents about what clothes their children should wear during each season. Some parents bought clothing that was too large, not warm enough, or unsuitable for humidity, snow, or rain. Buying the wrong outfit and having to buy something else instead also proved expensive. The kindergarten kept a small supply of clothes for loan, but found that these were often lost and not returned. At the point of transition from one season to the next, the kindergarten always mentioned something like 'now is the time for warmer clothes'. Such instructions were only given in Norwegian, however, and would not have helped those parents who were less fluent in the language. Though they initially blamed the parents, staff eventually realized that it was their job to educate them and so re-assumed that responsibility. They developed pictures of correct clothing for different seasons and guided the parents about sizes and fabric and even where they could buy most economically without compromising on quality. They developed pictures of individual items – gloves, socks, or woollen longs, for example – to indicate when, and what items of clothing were missing from a child's outfit. These pictures were kept on the child's individual shelf. This practice was used for all children, as a reminder to the parents. Again, the staff – and the school – made the transition from being problem-oriented to finding practical solutions that took cultural and linguistic differences into account.

Competence development

In the last few years, both kindergartens in this study have participated in a local branch of a national project to develop competence. The project was developed in conjunction with the local university college and county governor and initiated by a national resource centre (NAFO). According to Norwegian authorities, the project was intended 'to help raise awareness and increase action competence among kindergarten staff so that all children have the opportunity to have their basic needs met'. Two or three employees from several kindergartens – including the two in this study – attended lectures and workshops on diversity issues at the local university college about four times a year. When they returned to their workplace, they tried to convey their experiences of these sessions to the rest of the staff. The participants in the project emphasized how much more conscious they became of children's linguistic development. Both kindergartens established Norwegian language groups for a small number of children, which contained some from ethnic minorities as well as Norwegian-speaking pupils. Some participants reported that developing work methods for minority children helped strengthen the educational work they were doing generally.

People saw positive changes; however, staff disagreed about the extent to which the project increased their cultural competence. On returning to work, some did not change their manner of working in ways that were notably different. Interviews and fieldwork observations highlighted an ideology inherent in some daily practices that stressed the importance of 'treating everybody the same'. Such thinking does not take the individual into account, nor does it see the need to provide diverse teaching to a group of diverse learners. Observations made during the fieldwork support our interpretation that some of the staff's practice is unreflective and without a clear foundation in educational thinking. The Danish pedagogue Ûzeyr Tireli (2006) supports this interpretation when he warns that an unreflective openness can lead to exclusion, despite the fact that 'in Danish schools and kindergartens, there is no doubt that in the educational area there is openness, helpfulness and a great willingness to create good relations with both children and adults among the ethnic minorities'.

Developing communication across language barriers

The minority parents and children in this study came from many different countries – Somalia, Nigeria, Iran, Iraq, Thailand, and the Philippines – and spoke a variety of languages, although many were born in Norway. The length of time that parents had been in the country varied, as did their ability in the language and their familiarity with Norwegian society and kindergartens. Some parents therefore needed an interpreter while others did not. The kindergarten's practice was to invite an interpreter to assist with start-up conversations with new minority parents, to other priority conversations, and to parent meetings. In day-to-day contexts at the kindergarten, however, interpreters or bilingual assistants were seldom available. Outside larger cities, many communities do not typically have access to interpreters, bilingual teachers, or even assistants with knowledge of the languages spoken in the local kindergarten. A telephone interpreter might be used at scheduled meetings but not in the everyday running of the kindergarten. This lack of a common language made it difficult for staff to inform parents about practical issues such as future plans, appropriate clothing, or activities that their children participated in during the day. Several employees were frustrated by these communication barriers. They wanted to tell the minority parents what their child had been involved in, as they did with the other parents.

The staff responded to these linguistic barriers in different ways. Some chose to avoid making contact with the minority parents, leaving that to colleagues whom they believed had more experience with bilingual communication. One of them admitted: 'We may have a tendency to withdraw from what is difficult.' The staff's insecurity regarding communication was highlighted in their interactions with two quite different mothers. One had few Norwegian language skills but tried to make herself understood nonetheless, while the other was more reserved and preferred to speak in English, a language that she had mastered more proficiently than Norwegian. The staff had good contact with the first mother – who often came into the kitchen in the morning, had a cup of tea, and exchanged a few words – but with the second they felt compelled to speak in English, a language in which many lacked confidence. Although the first mother spoke in imperfect Norwegian, the staff were able to converse with her in their own language, and thus feel less uncertain about speaking with her. With the second mother, the staff felt some uncertainty about having to communicate in English, even though they had learnt it in primary and secondary school. In reality, however, this may not have been a barrier (as they had anticipated) but a starting point for them to understand the challenges that minority parents face with a foreign language. Nevertheless, staff mostly avoided situations where they had to struggle in a foreign language.

In one kindergarten, teaching staff sometimes asked the kitchen assistant to speak to minority parents, as she spoke better English than they did. While this solved the immediate problem of communication, staff with educational responsibility missed out on direct contact with multilingual parents. This affected minority parents and their children since they were not able to receive and offer information to the same degree as parents who were fluent Norwegian speakers. This type of practice is particularly problematic when a child first starts kindergarten, as both they and their parents require first-hand information from the staff if they are to feel at home.

In one instance, contact with one set of minority parents deteriorated. Speculating as to why, staff were eventually told that the family's application for asylum had been rejected. The parents' withdrawal was thus a consequence of their situation outside the kindergarten. Reflecting on this instance provided staff with valuable knowledge about the uncertainty that asylum-seekers face, and it became a lasting lesson for them.

In another instance the staff were frustrated by a minority father, whose failure to deliver his children within the scheduled time created problems for the kindergarten's planned activities. The staff thought him sloppy, until they discovered that he worked evening shifts and only returned from work at 2 o'clock in the morning. Sharing information like this with the members of staff allowed them to understand his situation, even though it continued to create practical challenges.

Such examples emphasize the importance of having time to reflect on experiences and share knowledge. The process increases contact and improves understanding between staff and parents. Both kindergartens eventually organized a Diversity Group where selected staff members from all sections met and discussed the diversity work that the kindergarten was doing, shared experiences and challenges, analysed particular cases or incidents concerning the minority children, and occasionally interacted with a guest who introduced a related subject.

International Day celebration – exotification and making a difference

In one of the activities celebrating International Day, the Hill kindergarten focused on the different cultures and languages present in the kindergarten and invited all the parents to attend the celebrations. Food from different countries was served – often made by parents from these countries – and there were exhibitions of maps, flags, information, objects, and clothes. Also on display were posters with words and phrases in the languages spoken in the kindergarten. One year all staff members were asked to work with the minority-ethnic parents to gather information about the countries that they came from and about any artefacts that they had. Some staff members tried to avoid this task, and asked a colleague whom they felt had more experience of dealing with minority parents to cover for them. Since one of the project's goals was to move beyond avoidance strategy (thereby providing all staff members with a richer intercultural experience), such attempts were not accepted by the educational leaders. After initial protests, both staff and parents became enthusiastic and thought that the idea was exciting and fun. Since the staff needed to talk to the parents in order to prepare for the exhibition, asking them to bring food or provide words and phrases for the language display, they were forced to overcome their own uncertainty and try to communicate as best they could. Working with the parents triggered the process of self-reflection and was important for everyone involved. The staff felt that it reduced their anxiety about communicating with minority parents since the occasion that had brought them together was fun and celebratory and everyone had participated actively. Feedback from parents confirmed their appreciation that the kindergarten had presented information about their countries of origin. One member of staff summarizes the experience thus: 'First of all we noticed that the kids were very proud ... And they were concerned to show their parents, they pulled them into their own section to show them ... So it was really, really fun to work with .... We learned a lot, those of us who work here as well.'

The nature of the impact that organizing International Day had is open to question. On the one hand there is a danger that celebrations become happenings – once-only events that have a minimal effect on the everyday life of the kindergarten. There is also a danger of exotification: concentrating on differences may reinforce what is considered normal– i.e. Norwegian – and thus maintain borders, cultural distance, and the process by which one group is ranked above another. On the other hand, however, including parents in preparations allows the staff to appreciate their diverse backgrounds. The children were proud to introduce their parents to the kindergarten and the staff felt compelled to tackle communication problems and overcome their anxiety. The time that they spent together preparing for the day may lead to improved relations between staff and parents with a first language other than Norwegian, reducing distance between them and making their day-to-day communication easier.

One informant expressed the long-term effects of International Day in this way:

> Because we focus on them [minority ethnic parents], they feel even more noticed and welcome. ... We discovered that some parents who *before* [International Day] delivered their child in the outer hall *now* they came into the locker room. They passed the threshold of coming into the department or the kitchen. That is a

big leap, and it presented quite a challenge because the further they came into the department, the more we talked with them and they had to respond ... It was so good to see. And they sort of lit up when we met elsewhere too, saluted and waved from a distance.

This observer still differentiates between 'us' and 'them', but nonetheless celebrates a development where the borders between the two are reduced, both linguistically and in relation to the use of space in the kindergarten.

Staff members reported that some of the minority-ethnic parents appeared at more meetings and events in the kindergarten after this. The staff also found that, despite language differences, it was easier to communicate because they knew each other better and the parents worried less about making mistakes. They used more body language; there was more laughter and smiles when they tried to communicate. This example does not suggest that a common language is unimportant, but it does emphasize how crucial it is to maintain positive contact and closeness between staff and parents, and to build on existing communication channels.

Conclusions and implications

In both the kindergartens in this study, attitudes among the kindergarten staff towards cultural diversity among children and parents were changing. While a clear tendency to distinguish between 'us' (Norwegians) and 'them' (non-Norwegians) stressed the differences between these two groups, the picture became more complex when staff negotiated interactions with children and parents from minority-ethnic groups. There was an impression that the staff in both kindergartens had steadily developed an overall positive attitude towards cultural diversity. They came to see the cultural complexity among the children as an asset to all in the kindergarten, and the tendency to simply divide groups on the basis of language or culture was waning. Several staff members appeared to be moving from a state of anxiety and reluctance to what may be called a normalization. Although they initially tended to regard minority children and their parents as 'special', focusing on the differences between majority and minority, most of the staff now seemed to treat each child as an individual, regarding those of both majority and minority backgrounds as all part of the kindergarten – and not as representative of any particular group. The staff's ways of thinking and acting indicated a shift towards an institution where cultural differences were just part of many differences.

A fundamental basis for these changes in practice was the experience of daily contact with children and parents from minority backgrounds.

Whatever preconceptions the staff might have had, over time their interaction with parents and children provided frequent examples of how all children and parents are unique, be they from a minority or a majority background. Even though there were challenges with communication, over time the staff found that the parents were 'just like us', as one put it. Formal and informal discussions and dialogues between the kindergartens' employees as they gained experience helped to change their views. The International Day described above illustrates how, when staff who were very sceptical were coerced into making contact, the result for everyone involved was amazing: the employees felt it was easier to communicate with the minority parents, while the parents and children felt that they were seen, acknowledged, and made more welcome. This did not stem from improved linguistic prowess, but from the mutual contact and rapport that they managed to establish. Getting to know each other seemed to enhance the staff's understanding of the parents' situation and made them try harder still to communicate with the parents. This was certainly a positive move in the direction of social justice and empowerment for a diverse group of children. It allowed them to be seen as complex individuals, not defined merely by assumed characteristics of similarities and differences based on the staff's preconceptions.

However, before they could try to bridge the communication gap, the employees had to work hard to overcome their own anxiety and resistance. To tackle these issues, they used different strategies, some of them counterproductive, like the avoidance strategy. Their educational plans and projects, however, and continuous competence development work succeeded in improving communication between parents and staff over time. This philosophical turn-around and a subsequent change of practice seemed to affect most staff members through their own experiences and the discussions and reflections on them among the staff. In addition, the information meetings with the reception centre seemed essential in diminishing their initial anxiety. This educational input was followed up with training courses at the local university college and in-house competence development and projects, all aimed at increasing the staff's 'diversity competence'.

The kindergartens' administrative and educational leaders also put pressure on staff to acquire the skills needed to work well with the diverse groups of children. Many staff found the cultural and linguistic diversity in their everyday work positive and rewarding. But the study also detected resistance towards these changes from some of the staff who found the changes too demanding. The implication of these complex findings is that working towards affirming cultural diversity in the kindergarten, whether among children or staff, is a continuous process. Diversity competence development must be perpetual, and leadership must continue to focus on issues of social justice and empowerment. Only then can room for cultural diversity be secured and a learning environment provide social justice to all children.

Notes

[1] The study was conducted as a part of the project 'Daycare centres and change. Inclusion in practice' (2008–11), financed by the Norwegian Research Council and led by Professor Randi Dyblie Nielsen, NTNU NOSEB.

[2] In this chapter the term 'minority' is used to refer to different groups of immigrant background and 'majority' to refer to persons or groups of ethnic-Norwegian background. At times the term 'children from minority backgrounds' is used, but for simplicity it is sometimes shortened to 'minority children'. I am aware that this is not customary or even regarded as acceptable in all countries. In the Norwegian context, immigrants and refugees constitute a minority in numbers, and this is what 'minority' is intended to signify in this study.

References

Barth, F. (1969) *Ethnic Groups and Boundaries: The social organization of culture difference*. Oslo: Universitetsforlaget.

Cummins, J. (1996) *Negotiating Identities: Education for empowerment in a diverse society,* (revised edition). Ontario, California: California Association for Bilingual Education.

Douglas, M. (2002) *Purity and Danger: An analysis of the concept of pollution and taboo; with a new preface by the author*. London: Routledge.

Fanon, F. (1986) *Black Skin, White Masks*. London: Pluto Press.

Gullestad, M. (1996) *Imagined Childhoods: Self and society in autobiographical accounts*. Oslo: Scandinavian University Press.

— (2002) *Det Norske Sett med Nye øyne: Kritisk analyse av norsk innvandringsdebatt*. Oslo: Universitetsforlaget.

— (2006) *Plausible Prejudice: Everyday experiences and social images of nation, culture and race*. Oslo: Universitetsforlaget.

Hall, S. (1996) 'Who needs identity?' In Hall, S. and Du Gay, P. (eds) *Questions of Cultural Identity*. London: Sage.

Hauge, A.M. (2007) *Den Felleskulturelle Skolen*, 2nd ed. Oslo: Universitetsforl.

Lauritsen, K. (2011) 'Barnehagen i kulturell endring - tilpassing og motstand'. In Bae, B. and Korsvold, T. (eds) *Barndom, Barnehage, Inkludering*. Bergen: Fagbokforlaget.

Migdal, J.S. (2004) *Boundaries and Belonging: States and societies in the struggle to shape identities and local practices*. Cambridge: Cambridge University Press.

Ministry of Education and Research (2006) 'Framework Plan for the Content and Tasks of Kindergartens'. Online. www.regjeringen.no/upload/KD/Vedlegg/ Barnehager/engelsk/Framework_Plan_for_the_Content_and_Tasks_of_ Kindergartens_2011.pdf (accessed 13 March 2012).

Statistics Norway (2010) 'Children in kindergartens: Final figures'. Online. www. ssb.no/english/subjects/04/02/10/barnehager_en/ (accessed 13 March 2012).

— (2011) 'Population, Immigrants and Norwegian-born to Immigrants, by Country Background. 1970–2011'. Online. www.ssb.no/english/subjects/02/01/10/innvbef_en/tab-2011-04-28-06-en.html (accessed 13 March 2012).

Staunæs, D. (2004) *Køn, Etnicitet, og Skoleliv.* Fredriksberg: Forlaget Samfundsliteratur.

Tireli, Ü. (2006) *Pædagogik og Etnicitet: Dialogisk pædagogik i et multikulturelt samfund.* Copenhagen: Akademisk forlag.

Chapter 3

Towards flexible pre- and primary education in multicultural contexts? An example of collaborative action research in Finland

Heini Paavola, Kaisa Kopisto,
Annu Brotherus, and Fred Dervin

Like many national and international declarations – e.g. the United Nations Convention on the Rights of the Child (1989), the UNESCO Salamanca Statement (1994), the Charter of Luxembourg (1996), and the United Nations Convention on the Rights of Persons with Disabilities (2006) – the Constitution of Finland emphasizes equity and equality (731/1999, 6 § 2 mom). In the sphere of education this translates as equal opportunities, irrespective of domicile, sex, economic situation, or linguistic and cultural background. There are no gender-specific school services in Finland. Basic education is free of charge and includes instruction, school materials, school meals, healthcare, dental care, commuting, special needs education, and remedial teaching (see Finnish National Board of Education (FNBE) at www. oph.fi). This chapter looks at equity and equality in Finnish multicultural pre- and primary education.

A few words outlining basic education in Finland are needed. Basic education includes one year of preschool education for children aged 6, followed by comprehensive and compulsory education for all children aged 7–16. Preschool (or pre-primary education, as it is referred to in the National Core Curriculum) is provided in day-care centres or preschool classes operating in connection with comprehensive schools. Municipalities are obliged to provide preschool education but participation is voluntary. Almost 98 per cent of children in Finland are involved in preschool education (Opetus- ja kulttuuriministeriö [Ministry of Education], 2012).

The path from preschool to school should form a unified whole. This has been taken into consideration in the curricula of preschool and primary school education. According to the *Core Curriculum for Pre-Primary Education* (2010), the aim of preschool education is to help children develop learning skills and a positive self-image, and to acquire basic skills, knowledge, and capabilities in different areas in accordance with their age and abilities. In the *Core Curriculum for Basic Education* (2004), the focus of education is on growth, learning, and the development of a balanced identity, so that children develop the skills and knowledge that they will need in life. Education also aims to enhance a child's readiness to study 'lifelong' and to turn them into active citizens in a democratic society. Finally, education should strengthen the language and cultural identity of every pupil, as well as the development of their first language (*Core Curriculum for Basic Education*, 2004).

The project we present in this chapter, the 'Flexible Preschool and School', was a three-year collaborative action research and development project (2007–10) funded by the Helsinki City Education Department. Its main purpose was to develop and test new models and methods in preschool and primary classes (Years 1 and 2) so as to enhance children's general learning skills – especially their social, linguistic, working, and thinking skills, and their learning and working habits – and thus enable them to progress from preschool to elementary school within two to four years. Accordingly, the Education Department and Social Services Department of the City of Helsinki established the project in two day-care centre school units[1] in 2007. A third unit was added to the project in August 2008. Our research project was also connected to the units' ongoing development work. Its aims were formulated in collaboration with various employees in both the education and social service departments of the City of Helsinki. Representatives from the day-care centres and schools were involved in the project steering committee.

All the units involved in the project were located in areas of Helsinki with the highest concentration of migrants. Mass immigration is a recent phenomenon in Finland and has increased steadily every year since the beginning of the new millennium. In 2011 approximately 30,000 people immigrated to Finland (Statistics Finland, 2012) – 3,000 more than the previous year. In some of the preschool and school classes that we worked with, the proportion of immigrant pupils was over 50 per cent. For these reasons every unit received 'positive discrimination funding' for the provisions needed, such as differentiation and extra support for special education. The project classes[2] were also resourced with special education teachers (from autumn 2007 until spring 2010 in two units, and from autumn 2008 until spring 2010 in one unit) and with special kindergarten teachers (all three units from spring 2009 until spring 2010).

The data were collected in three selected preschool classes and three primary school classes by means of collaborative action research. Every class had pupils with special needs and approximately 30 per cent of the pupils were from immigrant backgrounds. In the first phase of the project (2008–09) three of us – Kaisa Kopisto, Annu Brotherus, and Heini Paavola – made ourselves known in the units and familiarized ourselves with their physical and pedagogical environment, staff, and children. We also conducted preliminary surveys and initial interviews with staff and made video recordings and observations of lessons in pre- and primary school classes. The learning environments were also photographed. In the second phase of the project (2009–10) we continued collecting data, but the focus was on specific informant pupils (ct.1) and their activities, experiences, and opinions, rather than on the staff working in the schools. During the project there were four assessment days, in which the work of the staff and pupils was reflected upon and evaluated and plans for the future were made.

This chapter presents a case study that looks at the influence that collaborative action research had on both the teachers and the pupils. This approach is unique to the Finnish context as it is one of only a few attempts to promote cooperation between researchers and practitioners in dealing with such issues. Moreover, the fact that it examines the experiences of both the children and the staff – as participants in and promoters of flexible education, respectively – marks it out as an important departure from the typical one-way approach, which concentrates on only one, rather than both, of these groups.

To present our study in context, we begin this chapter by outlining the problems that surround multicultural education and inclusion in Finland. Next we describe the design of the Flexible Preschool and School project, including its methods and action research strategies, then turn our attention to the main findings. We analyse the informant children's involvement in pre- and primary school activities as well as our interviews with them. Using these results we also examine their experiences of these activities and any opinions that they might have formed. Staff interviews are then reviewed so as to consider their experiences, and the chapter ends with a few remarks about the learning environments.

What is the multicultural in education?

In the last few years Finnish education has attracted worldwide attention for its excellent results in several international rankings, such as the

OECD Programme for International Student Assessment, which surveys 15-year-olds in industrialized countries (Sahlberg, 2011). As a result, many researchers and decision-makers are visiting the country to investigate the 'Finland Phenomenon'. Very few – if any at all – ever mention the state of multicultural education, much less the ideas of inclusion and social justice in relation to the 'Other' (Dervin *et al.*, 2012). Like most European countries, Finland has recently experienced increased immigration so discussion about these concepts is essential in order to introduce our project.

While multicultural education is not new in Finnish scholarship and practices (see Talib *et al.*, 2009), there is no shared consensus about what it actually means, what it entails, and how it should be worked upon and implemented (Holm and Londen, 2010). Policy analyses of the latest National Curriculum and official educational documents shows that notions such as 'intercultural' or 'multicultural' are often used without heed to their complex implications (Riitaoja, in publication) – as if they were unambiguous. Yet researchers have shown how multifaceted and indeed problematic these notions are (Abdallah-Pretceille, 2003; Dervin *et al.*, 2012; Dervin and Keihäs, 2012).

Current educational policies tend to assume that the multicultural refers exclusively to the 'Other' – i.e. certain categories of migrant pupils such as refugees. In doing so, they obscure the fact that many Finnish youths also represent diversity. The idea that Finland's is a highly homogeneous 'culture' is widespread, even in research, but it paints an essentialist and robot-like image of the country and its people. The particular obsession with this image probably relates to the use, overuse, and abuse of the 'old and tired' concept of culture (Breidenbach and Nyíri, 2009: 10), which is omnipresent but rarely criticized. In Finnish education, this concept plays a major part in discussions about the inclusion of multicultural – or, in current parlance, those *diverse* – pupils. In these discussions, the cultural quite often cancels out other aspects of identity such as gender, generation, social class, and language. Yet the multicultural is always a point of view, a way of analysing interactions; it is not 'a given of nature' (Abdallah-Pretceille, 2003). Placing these considerations in the context of Finland's increased migration, this chapter uses the multicultural to refer to pupils beyond the single definition of a foreign culture – i.e. any pupil in the units under scrutiny.

Problematizing inclusion and pre- and primary education

As in other Nordic countries, Early Years education and preschool in Finnish pedagogy stress child participation, democracy, autonomy, and freedom (*Core Curriculum for Pre-Primary Education*, 2010; Jensen, 2009). This can be demanding for many children, who are seen both as full agents in their own learning processes and as competent individuals who are urged to engage actively in their environments (Brooker, 2005). In Nordic countries, it has repeatedly been argued that children – whether from migrant backgrounds or not – can find it difficult to adapt to what is required of them, and struggle to perform linguistically, socially, and academically in schools (Griffin, 2008: 110; Jensen, 2009). Many scholars (e.g. Brooker, 2005; Robinson and Jones Díaz, 2006; Yelland *et al.*, 2008: 82) assert that educators should focus on collaborative ways of knowing and learning that could include values and knowledge other than those of the majority. For example, reducing competitive individualism in preschools and schools would provide every child with a genuine opportunity to be included, to participate, and to be a member of the school community. This thinking is central to the rationale of our project.

For Adrian Holliday (2010: 39), the list-like and descriptive approach to cultures – Finns are… Russians do… – presented and used in education is extremely ideological and too static to allow multiple identities and 'diverse diversities' (Dervin, 2012) to be appreciated. This approach also relates to a further misconception – what Dervin (*ibid.*) has labelled a 'differentialist bias'. Cultural difference is often the sole basis of multicultural education in Finland. For Anne Phillips (2010: 20), cultural difference tends to lead to cultural hierarchy: 'There are said to be "better" and "worse", "more advanced" and "more backward" cultures'. This approach ignores the fact that 'each of us live in a web of cultural references and meanings' (*ibid.*: 61), which makes it difficult to define a difference as national, ethnic, or cultural, for example.

By insisting on 'walling in' pupils to certain cultures and geographical spaces – again, 'a Somali does this', 'a Chinese person behaves like that' – educationalists can easily impede inclusion in schools and societies. We argue that, by privileging such approaches, inclusion contributes to 'subconscious' exclusion by placing boundaries between people and thus creating hierarchies. The 'Other' is never allowed to play an active role in education – and, indirectly, in society as a whole – as discourses of 'our' culture and 'their' culture place them in a powerless position (Breidenbach and Nyíri, 2009: 340). Some of the differences that we define and use in our work with immigrant children, or even with second- or third-generation migrants, can be extremely ideological. For example, the idea that Asian pupils are collectivist and have very little autonomy is a dangerous bias, since such ideas are based on values to which we attach very positive elements. Holliday (2010), for example, has shown that behind the collectivist argument lies an old stereotype that equates collectivity, community, and the group to being 'less intelligent'. It is quite revealing that in Finland – and elsewhere – special needs education and multicultural education are amalgamated, as if the 'Other' was always 'deficient'. In education, the widespread idea of 'respecting other cultures' is ambiguous and potentially exclusionary: who does one turn to – the authorities? – for information about the cultural characteristics of the 'Other' and what role are they allowed to play in answering these questions?

This potential for exclusion is why social justice for all is imperative in education, especially if it allows both teachers and pupils to move beyond these difficulties. The development of complex identities – as opposed to 'walled in' identities – that go beyond established national, linguistic, or religious distinctions needs to be supported in pre- and primary education. This process challenges teachers, asking them to provide an inclusive learning environment and encourage every child in their tasks. Having diverse daily practices and learning strategies and reflecting critically on their former routines are all fundamental requirements. Finally, standardized measures – often used in preschool settings in Finland – should be avoided, as they can lead to situations where differences between children are seen only as problems and their similarities are sidelined (Yelland *et al.*, 2008). The project we report on in this chapter attempted to take these criticisms of multicultural education and inclusion into account.

Applying collaborative action research: design, methods, and data

To make our case study more coherent, we present the entire project: its design, its methods, and the data we collected.

The project was organized in two separate phases. The first phase set out to describe the structures, models, and instructional approaches used in the units and the learning environments in the classes. Our project also focused on the structures and methods that staff in each unit developed and tested to create functional and flexible education practices. One of our main aims was to advance those working models and methods that enabled all children – including migrant children and children with special needs – to move from preschool to primary school within two to four years, without transferring to special education. To define the project's focus and aims more precisely, we began with preliminary surveys and interviews, and created Figure 3.1 to describe the project's design. The research questions were focused on the children, teaching staff, and environment (Figures 3.1 and 3.2).

DESIGN OF THE PROJECT

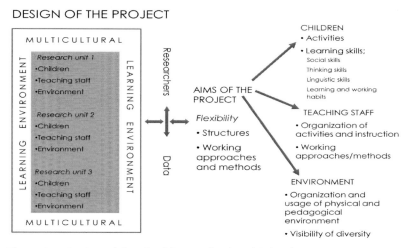

Figure 3.1: Design of the Flexible Preschool and School project

The project was conducted in three units (preschool groups and classes in Year 1 and Year 2). The research participants were preschool children and their kindergarten teachers, special kindergarten teachers, pupils in classes 1 and 2, their class teachers, and special teachers. One unit also had a teacher who taught Finnish as a second language, and who worked as a team member during the project. To capture the children's perspectives in 2009 and 2010 we focused on certain informant children who had been chosen by the units' staff. From every unit we selected one child from an immigrant background, one child with special educational needs, and one child who was neither from an immigrant background nor had special needs. The total number of children participating in the project from 2008 to 2010 was 159. Table 3.1 presents information about the units, the staff, and the informant children.

In the project we took a collaborative action research approach, which allowed us to cooperate with the teachers to improve their teaching practices and help them overcome the isolation they sometimes experienced (Ainscow *et al.*, 2004). We were also interested in the children's learning. Figure 3.2 shows how the project proceeded in cycles from 2008 to 2010, and also indicates how we focused on targets and used data-gathering methods during each cycle.

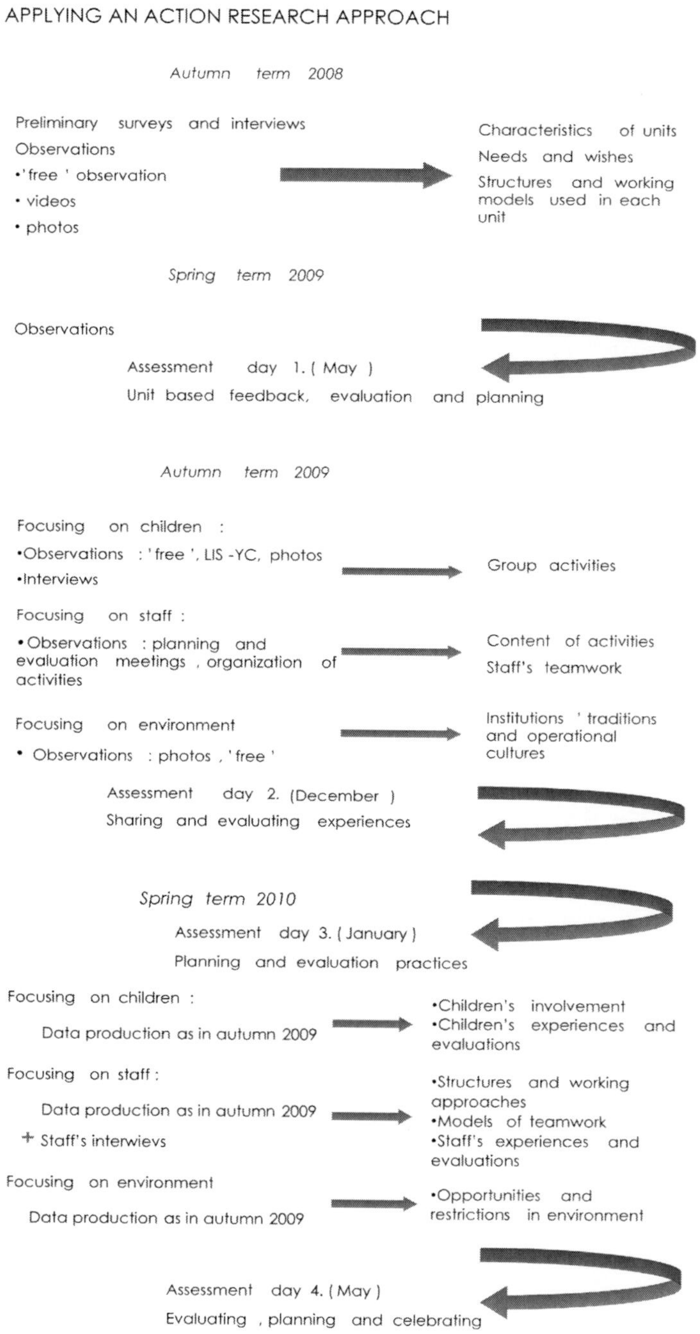

APPLYING AN ACTION RESEARCH APPROACH

Autumn   term   2008

Preliminary   surveys   and   interviews
Observations
•'free ' observation
• videos
• photos

Characteristics   of units
Needs   and   wishes
Structures   and   working
models   used   in   each
unit

Spring   term   2009

Observations

Assessment   day 1. (May)
Unit based   feedback,   evaluation   and planning

Autumn   term   2009

Focusing   on   children   :
•Observations   : 'free ', LIS -YC, photos
•Interviews

Group   activities

Focusing   on   staff :
• Observations   : planning   and
evaluation   meetings , organization   of
activities

Content   of activities
Staff's   teamwork

Focusing   on   environment
• Observations   : photos , 'free '

Institutions ' traditions
and operational
cultures

Assessment   day 2. (December)
Sharing and evaluating   experiences

Spring   term 2010
Assessment   day 3. (January)
Planning and evaluation   practices

Focusing on children :
   Data production as in autumn 2009

•Children's   involvement
•Children's   experiences   and
evaluations

Focusing on staff :
   Data production as in autumn 2009
 + Staff's interwievs

•Structures   and working
approaches
•Models   of teamwork
•Staff's experiences   and
evaluations

Focusing on environment
   Data production as in autumn 2009

•Opportunities   and
restrictions   in environment

Assessment   day 4. (May)
Evaluating , planning and celebrating

Figure 3.2: Action research process, targets, and data-gathering methods during cycles

Table 3.1: Research units, staff, and informant children in each unit

INFORMANTS

Research unit	Teaching staff	Preschool groups and primary classes	Informant children
Unit 1	•2 kindergarten teachers •1 special kindergarten teacher •2 class teachers •1 special teacher •Finnish as a second language teacher	*From 2008 to 2010* Preschool group 1st grade 2nd grade	•Girl/preschool •Boy/immigrant,1st grade •Boy/special needs, 2nd grade
Unit 2	•1 kindergarten teacher •1 special kindergarten teacher •2 class teachers •1 special teacher	*From 2008 to 2010* Preschool group 1st grade 2nd grade	•Boy/preschool, special needs •Boy/1st grade •Boy/immigrant, 2nd grade
Unit 3	•2 kindergarten teachers •1 special kindergarten teacher •2 class teachers •1 special teacher	*2008 - 2009* Preschool group 1st grade *2009 - 2010* Preschool group 1st grade 2nd grade	•Boy/immigrant, preschool •Girl/special needs, 1st grade •Boy/2nd grade

We planned the schedule and data-gathering methods at the start of the project. Throughout the process we repeatedly evaluated and specified our targets and methods, both individually and in collaboration with the staff. The data were gathered by three researchers who worked mainly in pairs. One of us made videotape recordings and took photographs; another observed the children using the Leuwen Involvement Scale for Young Children (LIS-YC); two interviewed the children; and all of us interviewed and observed the staff.

To gauge their level of involvement in the project activities, we used the LIS-YC process indicator for observing the children. The LIS-YC has five different levels for recording the intensity of a child's involvement. Level 1 represents a lack of activity; on Level 2 a child's activity is constantly interrupted; on Level 3 a child is more or less continuously concentrating on an activity; on Level 4 their activity includes intensive moments; and on Level 5 the child is totally immersed in an activity. To us, a child who is involved in an activity has a large interest in what he or she is doing, and the child works intensively with persistence, energy, and passion. His or her involvement is observable and can be recognized in facial expressions and bodily movements (Laevers, 1997: 3, 8–16). The nine informant children were observed between 9 and 19 times each, which brought the total of three-minute observations to 120. To make our measurements more reliable we also photographed the informant children during our observations. The data were then analysed as follows: we counted the averages for every child, group, and research unit and, finally, for the whole dataset.

We also conducted thematic interviews with our informant children to explore their experiences and evaluations about the activities they had participated in. As analytical units we used the children's verbal discourses. Since the children were young and, in some cases, had only limited linguistic skills, the unit could be only one word (Brotherus, 2004: 70–74; Cavanagh, 1997; Kopisto *et al.*, 2011: 48–9).

General discussions with staff occurred frequently and we also organized semi-structured interviews in spring 2010. Each occupational group had their own interview, based on questions given to members beforehand. Through our questions we encouraged them to evaluate and reflect on the whole project, as well as on their own aims and achievements. We also asked them to identify what could be improved and how those improvements could be made, and to structure the way in which they would develop their collective practices.

We videotaped routine activities and photographed the physical learning environments. From the photographs we produced photomaps – posters made up of selected pictures – to provide a holistic view of each unit's physical environments and to compare the units' similar and unique features (Brotherus and Kopisto, 2005: 80–81; Collier, 2002: 54–6). We wanted to see how the environments compared in terms of the possibilities and restrictions that they presented and whether multiculturalness – that is, diverse diversities – was present in the physical learning environments and also how it was presented.

Main findings

This chapter does not provide answers to all of our research questions, nor does it reflect on important ethical issues (see Kopisto *et al.*, 2011). Rather, we concentrate here on the organization and content of the flexible activities in each unit, the children's involvement in these activities, and their opinions and wishes about their activities and learning. We also present staff evaluations about the project and some of the main points about the physical learning environments.

Organization and content of the flexible pre- and primary education in the units

The project's activities were organized and named differently in each unit.

In Unit 1 the activities were called Flexible Days. Children from pre- and primary classes were placed in four mixed groups who worked together for four weeks in certain subjects. Group work took place for two hours once a week. In the first phase of the project the main goals of the group work were to enhance the children's motor skills, emotional skills, and linguistic skills in Finnish, and in the second, to develop their interactive, emotional, and social skills. The groups remained the same for the whole school year. The school also had clubs that were organized by the special teachers, the aim of which was to enhance the children's mathematical and linguistic skills. In 2008 and 2009 a class teacher and a kindergarten special teacher jointly organized music lessons.

In Unit 2 the activities were called Project Days. From 2007 to 2008 the focus was on linguistic skills in Finnish and social skills. The children were put in five groups according to their skills. In autumn 2008 the staff switched the focus to language, the environment and nature studies, sports, and handicrafts. One group consisted of the pupils from class 2, two groups of pupils from class 1 and a preschool class, and one group of preschool pupils from classes 1 and 2. In the most heterogeneous group there were two teachers: a special teacher and a special kindergarten teacher. Owing to changes of staff in this unit the new plan was not successful, and in spring 2009 the unit returned to the way it had been working in 2007 and 2008.

In Unit 3 the activities were called Workshop Activities. This unit had used this type of working model before but, thanks to extra funding, now had the opportunity to set up the special teacher's school clubs. Children were placed in four groups according to their linguistic skills in Finnish, and the workshop activities were organized once a week. With the help of one teacher the groups focused on one theme for four weeks, at the end of which the teacher would change. The groups were kept the same throughout the school year. In this unit the children could also take part in weekly art and handicraft workshops. There were five workshops with different content, and every child had access to all of them throughout the school year.

The children's involvement in the activities

Our first interest was in the children's perceptions of the organized activities and how involved they were in them. The informant children were interviewed twice: in autumn 2009 and spring 2010. The interviews were always conducted by two researchers and were videotaped. There were questions about teachers, activities, and the learning environment, as well as about the children's own wishes for their learning. The interviews took half an hour on average.

Despite their differences, the outcomes between the units and among the preschool children and primary school children seemed quite similar. However, there were clear variations in the children's wishes and self-evaluations about their knowing and learning. When they spoke about their learning all the children referred to their teachers, mentioning that they were fond of them: teachers were nice, kind, and patient. The preschool children's wishes for knowing and learning were connected to goals that were not academic. Their wishes for learning related to playing, while the self-evaluations of their learning focused on their skilfulness in handicraft and physical education. One pupil in Unit 3 told us that she wanted to learn to read and write. A girl in Unit 1 wished to learn to draw like other pupils at the school, while a boy in Unit 2 stated in spring 2010 that 'I can't do everything'. It is important to note that the children could not separate the activities related to the project from other pre- and primary school activities. Only one girl (in Unit 1) mentioned that 'project days are fun, sometimes we do gym!'

The preference for learning of pupils in Years 1 and 2 were linked to subjects – mostly mathematics. Only one pupil told us that he enjoyed playing as much as he enjoyed schoolwork. Activities such as playing, taking part in games, and telling fairy tales took place outside school time. In autumn 2009, pupils in Years 1 and 2 could not differentiate between the project lessons and their normal schoolwork; but by spring 2010 they could. A boy in Unit 1 told us that project lessons were more fun than ordinary lessons, while another had noticed that 'it is different. Sometimes we have a competition.'

The children's involvement in the project's activities was analysed using the levels of the LIS-YC scale. Our findings reveal the following conclusions: the children in the pre- and primary classes were on average quite involved in the activities – a mean of 3.5; children not from an immigrant or special needs background received the highest scores – a mean of 3.9; the mean score of children from immigrant backgrounds was 3.4, while the children with special educational needs had the lowest score – 3.2.

The level of involvement was lowest among the preschool children – a mean of 3.16 – and highest among those in Year 1 – a mean of 3.9. The lowest mean scores – 2 and 2.3, respectively – in the entire target group were shown by a preschool boy who had limited skills in the Finnish language as well as special needs, and an immigrant boy in Year 1. At 3.5, the mean of Year 2 pupils was good but the degree to which the scores deviated among pupils was the highest of all – a deviation of 1.9.

The level of involvement in activities was especially high in the special teacher's school clubs in research Unit 1. High involvement scores were also achieved by most in the special teacher and kindergarten special teacher's joint learning sessions in research Unit 3. The goals of enhancing the children's linguistic and mathematical skills were attained, which proves that learning in small groups with the special teacher (and, in some cases, two teachers) was highly beneficial. The children had individualized learning targets and received special attention and, by learning in a familiar, supportive, and positive atmosphere, they were encouraged to work actively and express themselves.

The teachers' experiences and perceptions of the project

Perceptions at the beginning of the project

In the final group interviews in spring 2010, staff members recalled how confused they were when the collaborative action research project started. They related how their confusion was dispelled when the project began its development work with the researchers and when staff were presented with Figure 3.1:

> It was positive that the researchers came along. You started to understand our context and recognized also the socioeconomic background of our pupils. You have seen what we do in this school. It has encouraged us and made you and us closer... you know why we have chosen certain things, and where and why we have started.
>
> (Unit 1, class teacher, translated from Finnish by the authors)

All participants agreed that there had been a notable lack of support and knowledge, especially regarding immigrant children and children with special needs. The motivation to participate in the project is reflected in this quotation:

> Because a special teacher resource was included in this project, of course we wanted to participate. It was a starting point – there was a real need for this kind of project!
>
> (Unit 1, teacher of Finnish as a second language)

Hindering factors and cooperation among staff

Reflecting on what obstacles there had been during the project, staff in Unit 2 said that, because they had participated in another project, they found it hard to motivate themselves to take part in ours. During the project, this unit also experienced many changes of staff, which created problems for planning and evaluating the activities. Staff felt they were not given enough support by the principal and new teachers said that they were not given the information they needed to fully participate in the project. Changes in Unit 2 were shown clearly in their development work, where there was neither a follow-up period nor real progress made.

> The second year was a disaster! [There were] a lot of changes in the staff. Year 1 was terribly demanding, and we [in preschool class] also had a demanding group. We should have begun in a totally different way.
>
> (Unit 2, kindergarten teacher)

> The organization should have been better! Quite a flop! When we had already been involved in the project for two years, the principal should have managed the timetable matters so that the project would have been more feasible.
>
> (Unit 2, special teacher)

Staff from units 1 and 3, however, managed to develop co-planning and co-teaching practices and multi-professional teamwork. In these units the flexible timetable planned by the principals made multi-professional teamwork possible, as the teachers had extra time for planning and evaluating together.

> It is – I think – a very simple thing to organize. I devise the timetables and work into them the joint lessons to be used for cooperation.
>
> (Unit 1, principal)

That staff understood the meaning of multi-professional cooperation and implementing it within the school was one of the most worthwhile outcomes. In the pre- and primary classes, the teachers familiarized themselves with each others' work and came to appreciate each others' contribution more. Discussions between the professionals occurred more frequently and improved in quality, and cooperation became more systematic. The teachers also felt that multi-professional teamwork and co-teaching had a positive influence on their professional identities. Thanks to increased cooperation, the quality of teaching also improved, and this was reflected in the children's achievements. As one Unit 3 class teacher remarked, 'We have worked on our practices, and moved on from quantity to quality.'

Teachers' experiences and evaluations of achievements

When the units reflected on the project's results and achievements, Unit 1 expressed their satisfaction. According to the teacher, the decision to concentrate on mathematics and develop linguistic, social, and emotional skills was a sound and productive one. The unit also succeeded in developing working methods and practices that were useful in the teaching of Finnish as a second language. The most valuable outcome in Unit 2 was the development of pupils' oral and written expression. The teachers also felt that the children's individual needs were met, despite asserting that they could not develop any 'real' model or method during the project. According to the teachers in Unit 3, the children successfully achieved their learning goals, with particular credit given to the practices of co-teaching and working in small groups. Echoing those in Unit 1, the staff in Unit 3 stated that it was not only immigrant children and children with special needs who had benefited from the project, but that all children had gained from it. Teachers were especially pleased that those children who were at risk of dropping out of school could be provided with support. Both pre- and primary school children received the support they needed.

Both special teachers and class teachers felt that having a greater knowledge of pupils influenced home–school cooperation in a positive way. Class teachers felt that their working skills – especially in differentiation – had developed, and this made them more confident when meeting and interacting with parents. Special needs teachers regarded mutual cooperation between themselves as very fruitful. One special needs teacher from Unit 2 mentioned that 'The feedback from a colleague gives extra motivation to my work', while another, from Unit 3, reported that 'We have started to think more about those who need help, and to devote our resources to them'.

Learning environments

In every unit, the preschool and the school were placed in the same location. In units 1 and 3 pre- and primary classrooms were located close to one another, which facilitated cooperation. In Unit 2 the preschool was located on the ground floor and the primary classrooms on the first. This significantly hindered cooperation during the project, as the floors were like two different worlds, according to the teachers. 'They almost expect teachers from the school to start complaining about having to climb the stairs,' said one special needs teacher in Unit 2.

In every unit the planning of the learning environment was 'the last aspect to [be] concentrate[d] on'. Preschool classrooms resembled a home and were decorated with carpets, sofas, and flowers, among other items. Tables and chairs were set out in groups, materials were laid out on shelves and in cupboards, and they were often thematically arranged. Primary school classrooms were also typically arranged in a teacher-centred manner: the children's desks were arranged in rows or small groups and the teacher's table was placed at the front or the back of the room. Numbers and alphabets were displayed on the walls alongside the children's paintings and other artefacts. The pedagogical idea behind this environment was clear but the children's diversity was not taken into account. Both the equipment and the teaching and learning materials mostly reflected Finnish culture, while the children's paintings and handicrafts were often based on images associated with Finnishness, including nature and the country's animals, national celebration days, and national heroes.

Classrooms contained very few, if any, multicultural elements in terms of the pictures, posters, playing materials, or books that they contained. The only visual elements that acknowledged diversity were large wall maps, globes, and posters showing national flags. In one classroom in Unit 1 there were small items that referred to Sweden – Pippi Longstocking – and Russia – Matryoshka dolls – and a few characters such as Winnie the Pooh and Minnie Mouse that are known almost globally. 'We are not pleased with how the project has been made visible in our environment,' said a teacher of Finnish as a second language in Unit 1.

Conclusions and implications

This chapter has examined how the three-year Flexible Preschool and School project influenced six educational institutions in Helsinki. We have argued for a new understanding – and subsequent implementation – of the notions of multicultural education and inclusion, and described how some of these changes were taken into account in the conceptualization, implementation, and development of the project. In our analysis of the project we have highlighted the effects of our research on both the teachers and the pupils in the participating schools. Even though our collaborative action research with the teachers was short-term and somewhat limited, the staff noted positive improvements in the children's learning and social skills. It is therefore worth considering what more could be done with and for children if schools had greater flexibility and if multi-professional, cooperative working methods formed the basis of their practices.

Key results and implications for preschool and school education

First of all, our study allowed us to identify key factors in flexible education. It became clear that the special teacher's (and special kindergarten teacher's) role was crucial in all the units where the research took place. Their educational background had given them a deeper understanding of the children's differences and their knowledge was much appreciated in every unit. The special teachers also played a key role when the children were placed in differentiated groups or were grouped heterogeneously. They knew every child and could find a good solution for placement in activities. They also led the planning work and coordinated meetings with multi-professional staff.

Another important factor identified in the study was the central figure of the school principal, who can make multi-professional work happen in their preschool or school. It is for this reason that time for planning and evaluation needs to be acknowledged by principals and reserved in staff schedules. It is also the principal's responsibility to evaluate critically and creatively traditionally different operational cultures such as daily routines and practices, timetables, and planning and evaluation procedures. Such evaluation allows the principal to increase flexible, mutual, and productive working methods and possibilities that allow children to move smoothly from one institution to another. The motivation of staff is connected to circumstances in their working environment and directly affects children's learning achievements.

It is also important to bear in mind the children's uniqueness – and thus the idea of differentiation. These were significant starting points in the project and were taken into account when planning the activities. In the project lessons, children were placed in heterogeneous groups and the main aim was to develop their social skills. An interesting outcome from the heterogeneous groups was that loyalty towards each other was determined not by gender or age but by having the same culture and language group. This was especially apparent in those situations or lessons that were more 'informal' and included more free activities; for example, during group play, children with a similar 'cultural' background chose to play with each other. It may be interesting in a future study to investigate the reasons for this phenomenon: did the children belonging to minority linguistic and cultural groups feel more at ease about claiming their individual and collective identities in more informal situations or lessons? Did they feel they were outsiders or left alone in situations where they were not in the majority?

This points to an important issue regarding inclusion. Children who come to preschool with limited skills in the host language need special provision. During the special needs teacher's school clubs, the children were mostly grouped according to their age and to their skills in the Finnish language and in mathematics, and this had a positive impact on them. We believe that children should receive targeted teaching in the dominant language since this is the key to social interaction. At the same time, however, it is important for them to get to know their peers in their class and the school. Our project showed that when the children received extra individual attention and were given the chance to work with peer groups, their involvement increased and they were able to achieve their goals. Although involvement in the activities was generally high, the relatively low involvement of the preschool children raises the question of how suitable the aims of the activities and methods are for younger children. It is also important for preschool children to get a sense of the teachers, environments, lessons, and activities that they will encounter in primary school, as this may ease their transition.

We end with a few words about multicultural education. The teachers kept referring to the children's different backgrounds and uniqueness, yet the 'multicultural' was hardly noticeable in the classrooms. It was difficult for the teachers to understand that it is important for a child to identify with characters in a picture or a book, for example, or with playing material used in class. It is thus important for all children not to feel 'otherized' as this can affect not only their identity and self-image but also, importantly, their learning (Gay, 2005; Nieto, 2004). The teachers were devoted to the learning atmosphere and methods, yet the multicultural was not seen in the learning contents. One possible explanation for the absence of the 'renewed multicultural' is that the Finnish *Core Curriculum for Pre-Primary Education* (2010) and the *Core Curriculum for Basic Education* (2004) are based on certain canonical images of Finland, the Finns, and Finnish culture. The multicultural or the intercultural are just beginning to appear on the educational scene. This will, no doubt, in the near future lead to schools developing some of the ideas that we have put forward in this chapter, and making a contribution to easing all children's transition from pre- to primary education.

Notes
[1] In this chapter the word 'unit' refers to the combination of a day-care centre and a school chosen for the project. The criteria for choosing these units were the number of immigrant children they catered for and the location of the day-care centre and the school in the same precinct.
[2] By 'classes' we refer to both preschool groups and primary classes 1 and 2.

References
Abdallah-Pretceille, M. (2003) *Pour un Humanisme du Divers*. Paris: Economica.

Ainscow, M., Booth, T., and Dyson, A. (2004) 'Understanding and developing inclusive practices in schools: A collaborative action research network'. *International Journal of Inclusive Education*, 8 (2), 125–39.

Breidenbach, J. and Nyíri, P. (2009) *Seeing Culture Everywhere*. Washington: University of Washington Press.

Brooker, L. (2001) 'Interviewing children'. In Naughton, G.M., Rolfe, S.A., and Siraj-Blatchford, I. (eds), *Doing Early Childhood Research: International perspectives on theory and practice*. Buckingham: Open University Press.

Brooker, L. (2005) 'Learning to be a child: Cultural diversity and early years ideology'. In Yelland, N. (ed.), *Critical Issues in Early Childhood Education*. New York: Open University Press.

Brotherus, A. and Kopisto, K. (2005) 'Lapset matkalla esiopetuksessa ja esiopetuksesta alkuopetukseen'. In Hytönen, J. (ed.) *Esiopetuksen prosessi ja vaikutukse: Esiopetuksen toimivuus ja vaikuttavuus Helsingin kaupungissa vuosina 2001–2003.* (Soveltavan kasvatustieteen laitos 259). Helsinki: Helsingin yliopisto.

Brotherus, A. (2004) *Esiopetuksen Toimintakulttuuri Lapsen Näkökulmasta.* (Soveltavan kasvatustieteen laitos 251). Helsinki: Helsingin yliopisto.

Cavanagh, S. (1997) 'Content analysis: Concepts, methods, and applications'. *Nurse Researches*, 4, 5–16.

Collier, M. (2002) 'Approaches to analysis in visual anthropology'. In van Leeuwen, T. and Jewitt, C. (eds), *Handbook of Visual Analysis,* 2nd ed. London: Sage.

Core Curriculum for Basic Education (2004).

Core Curriculum for Pre-Primary Education (2010).

Dervin, F. (2012) *Impostures Interculturelles.* Paris: L'Harmattan.

Dervin, F., Gajardo, A., and Lavanchy, A. (eds) (2011) *Politics of Interculturality.* Newcastle: CSP

Dervin, F. and Keihäs, L. (2012) *Uusi Kulttuurienvälisyys.* Helsinki: Teos.

Dervin, F., Paatela-Nieminen, M., Kuoppala, M.-K., and Riitaoja, A.-L, (2012) 'Multicultural education in Finland – Renewed intercultural competences to the rescue?' *International Journal of Multicultural Education*, Fifth Anniversary Special Issue: Multicultural Education. Past, Present and Future.

Doverborg, E. and Pramling Samuelsson, I. (2001) *Att Förstå Barns Tankar: Metodik för barnsintervjuer,* 3rd ed. Stockholm: Liber.

Elliot, J. (1991) *Action Research for Educational Change.* Bristol, PA: Open University Press.

Erikson, E. (1969) *Identity, Youth and Crisis.* New York: Norton.

Gay, G. (2000) *Culturally Responsive Teaching: Theory, research and practice*: New York: Teachers College Press.

Griffin, S. (2008) *Inclusion, Equality and Diversity in Working with Children.* Harlow: Heinemann.

Holliday, A. (2010) *Intercultural Communication and Ideology.* London: Sage.

Holm, G. and Londen, M. (2010) 'The discourse on multicultural education in Finland: Education for whom?' *Intercultural Education*, 21 (2), 107–20.

Jensen, B. (2009) 'A Nordic approach to early childhood education (ECE) and socially endangered children'. *European Early Childhood Education Research Journal*, 17 (1), 7–21.

Kopisto, K., Brotherus, A., Paavola, H., Hytönen, J., and Lipponen, L. (2011) *Kohti joustavaa esi- ja alkuopetusta. Joustavan esi- ja alkuopetuksen tutkimus- ja kehittämishankkeen raportti.* Opetusviraston julkaisuja B1: 2011. Helsingin Kaupunki. Opetusvirasto.

Laevers, F. (ed.) (1997) *The Leuwen Involvement Scale for Young Children LIS-YC.* Handbook. Finnish edition by Airi Hautamäki. University of Helsinki. Department of Teacher Education. Continuing Training Center in Vantaa. Studia Paedagogica 14. Helsinki: Hakapaino.

Nieto, S. (2004). *Affirming Diversity: The sociopolitical context of multicultural education.* New York: Teachers College Press.

Opetus- ja kulttuuriministeriö [Ministry of Education] (2012) *Koulutus ja tutkimus vuosina 2011–2016. Kehittämissuunnitelma.* Opetus- ja kulttuuriministeriön julkaisuja 2012:1. Opetus- ja kulttuuriministeriö.

Phillips, A. (2010) *Gender and Culture.* Cambridge: Polity Press.

Riitaoja, A.L. 'Multiculturalism and social justice in schooling'. Unpublished PhD thesis.

Robinson, K.H. and Jones Díaz, C. (2006) *Diversity and Difference in Early Childhood Education: Issues for theory and practice.* Maidenhead: Open University Press.

Sahlberg, P. (2011) *Finnish Lessons: What can the world learn from educational change in Finland?* New York: Teachers College Press.

Statistics Finland (2012) 'Migration'. Online. www.stat.fi/til/muutl/index_en.html (accessed 27 November 2012).

Talib, M.-T., Loima, J., Paavola, H., and Patrikainen, S. (eds) (2009) *Dialogues on Diversity and Global Education.* Bern: Peter Lang.

Yelland, N., Lee, L., O'Rourke, M., and Harrison, C. (2008) *Rethinking Learning in Early Childhood Education.* Maidenhead: Open University Press.

Chapter 4

Supporting cultural and linguistic diversity in rural Manitoba: How one kindergarten–grade 6 school is rising to the challenge

Clea Schmidt

Introduction

Because of Canada's First Nations, Inuit, and Métis peoples, as well as a long history of immigration, and a large proportion of migrants in its population, cultural and linguistic diversity is common in the country's schools. Approximately 250,000 people migrate to Canada each year, making it a country with one of the largest foreign-born populations in the world. The Canadian government actively recruits immigrants to counter the country's declining birth rate and to boost its economy (Schmidt *et al.*, 2010).

Most newcomers to Canada have first languages and cultures that differ from those of the Anglo-Celtic immigrants who predominated until the 1970s (Reitz, 2011). While challenges facing non-white immigrant pupils who have English as an additional language (EAL) have been well studied, most of this research has concentrated on schools in urban centres such as Toronto, Montreal, and Vancouver (e.g. Lotherington, 2007). However, immigration in smaller towns and cities and in rural communities, particularly in the Prairie region of Canada, has been on the rise since 1997, when the federal government established provincial nominee programmes (Manitoba's was transitioned back to the jurisdiction of the federal government in 2012), which allowed individual provinces to set their own immigration targets and pursue their own recruitment agendas to respond to the needs of the regional labour market (Carter *et al.*, 2010). This new initiative aimed to address some of the shortcomings in the federal immigration programme, by expediting the immigration process for skilled workers and boosting economic and population growth in provinces that had not previously attracted high numbers of newcomers.

The research context

Abenberg School Division (ASD),[1] in rural Manitoba, the subject of the study presented in this chapter, experienced tremendous expansion in the proportion of children from immigrant families. From 1998 to 2008, the number of pupils with EAL increased from 23 to over 1,300 (Schmidt, 2011).[2] Of those immigrants with EAL, by far the largest group spoke German as their first language. Among this group, over 60 per cent had either High German (spoken in the upland areas of central and southern Germany) or Low German (spoken in the northern coastal and lowland regions of Germany). This predominance of one language group set ASD apart from the urban school divisions, where it was less usual to see such a high concentration of a single immigrant language, albeit one (in the case of German) with several variants. Some of the newcomers whose children attended ASD were originally from Germany, while others were Russian-born and arrived via Germany; others came from South American countries such as Paraguay and Bolivia. Most of these immigrants were Mennonite, and had been attracted to Canada for a variety of reasons, including the opportunity to own larger plots of land on which to raise their families and to maintain their religious and cultural beliefs among Canada's already well-established Mennonite community (Schmidt *et al.*, 2009).

The study described in this chapter analyses successful multilingual practices in Bonn Elementary School, a kindergarten–grade 6 school that caters for children from the age of 4 to 11. The school is situated in the small rural community of Bremen, which has a population of approximately 1,000. At the time of the study, Bonn Elementary School contained 360 pupils, of whom 30 per cent spoke Low German or High German as their first language, a percentage that was increasing (I: School Administrator, 01/20/09, p. 12).[3] By providing evidence of exemplary leadership and practices in relation to cultural and linguistic diversity, the case establishes the need to overtly identify challenges to student performance and home–school collaborations and strategically respond to these challenges. The research presented here offers insights for implementing effective practices and leadership with respect to other aspects of diversity such as gender, sexual orientation, religion, and special needs. It will be particularly relevant to smaller educational settings recently responding to student and family diversity.

Chapter overview

The chapter is grounded in critical multilingual and antiracist literature and theory. The methodology and context of the study are elaborated on and findings are analysed to show that the strategic hiring of staff who reflect the languages and cultures of students and families was important for implementing inclusive practices, defined in this case study as culturally and linguistically responsive pedagogy and family engagement. The chapter concludes with pedagogical and methodological insights for educators and researchers working in smaller settings that are new to a larger-scale immigration.

Literature review

Education for equity

Extensive research and literature on education emphasizes the need to provide appropriate academic and social support for immigrant learners with EAL so as to facilitate their success and that of their families (Cummins, 2007; Furman, 2008). Such support is often framed within an equity mandate. However, a myriad of influences – including the perception of linguistic and cultural diversity as a deficit (Cummins, 2003); racist attitudes towards immigrant learners on the part of white, Canadian-born teachers (Solomon *et al.*, 2005); 'diversity-related burnout' (Tatar and Horenczyk, 2003); and a perceived lack of preparedness (Schmidt, 2005) – impact on mainstream classroom teachers' responsiveness to the needs of their diverse learners. Subsequent challenges faced by newcomers in immigrant-receiving education systems have been well documented among learner and teacher populations (e.g. Schmidt, 2010); they include marginalization, challenges to successful academic and social integration, and exclusion from mainstream opportunities (e.g. Nieto, 2010). However, in spite of equity mandates and policies such as the Manitoba Action Plan for Ethnocultural Equity (Manitoba Education, Citizenship and Youth, 2006), which advocate more equitable treatment of immigrant learners and teachers, there is a failure to implement such policies in consistent and detectable ways (Schmidt and Block, 2010).

Discrepancy between student and teacher populations

Further obstacles stand in the way of equity for immigrant communities in Canadian education. First, the discrepancy between the growing diversity of student populations and the relative homogeneity of the teaching force is largely overlooked in policy and practice (Ryan *et al.*, 2009), including much teacher-education literature. Mainstream research in this area tends to assume that meeting the needs of students and families with EAL is simply a matter of providing additional professional development for the dominant white, middle-class female teaching force. The recruitment and retention of minority teachers is less frequently addressed (Bennett *et al.*, 2006; Carrier and Cohen, 2005; Kearney, 2008; Quiocho and Rios, 2000). As Failler (2009: 50) elaborates:

> For the dominant culture ... white identity is secured through the simultaneous exclusion and consumption of racialized others. That is, white, socially sanctioned practices such as racial profiling and segregation ensure that minorities and non-white immigrants never quite belong to the nation; the nation depends on possessing and exploiting these 'Others' to support its social and economic hierarchies, as well as its fantasies of itself as a multicultural, democratic state.

A comparative analysis of Canadian census data collected in 2001 and 2006 showed a growing disparity between the number of white teachers and ethnic minority teachers in Canada (Ryan *et al.*, 2009). Owing mostly to immigration, Canada saw a growth in its visible minorities from 13.4 per cent of the total population in 2001 to 16.2 per cent in 2006.[4] The proportion of visible minorities in the teaching force rose from 5.4 per cent of the teaching force in 2001 to just 6.9 per cent in 2006 (*ibid.*).

Given the systemic challenges to equitable educational opportunities for immigrant learners and teachers, exemplary practices like those found in Bonn Elementary School are important for demonstrating how schools can continue to challenge dominant discourses and practices in which immigrant students and families are perceived and treated as deficient.

Theoretical framework: critical pedagogy

A pedagogy that affirms multilingualism can be usefully framed within a critical theoretical context. As defined by Darder *et al.* (2009: 9):

> Critical pedagogy is fundamentally committed to the development and enactment of a culture of schooling that supports the empowerment of culturally marginalized and economically disenfranchised students. By doing so, this pedagogical perspective seeks to help to transform those classroom structures and practices that perpetuate undemocratic life. Of particular importance then is a critical analysis and investigation into the manner in which traditional theories and practices of public schooling thwart or

influence the development of a politically emancipatory and humanizing culture of participation, voice, and social action within the classroom. The purpose for this is intricately linked to the fulfillment of what Paulo Freire defined as our 'vocation'—to be truly humanized social (cultural) agents in the world.

Methodology and methods

In this study of Bonn Elementary School, the qualitative data presented are derived from a larger mixed-methods (Creswell and Plano Clark, 2007) study conducted in Abenberg School Division in 2008–09. The research questions explored are as follows: How did a school new to working with learners and families with English as an additional language (EAL) respond to the increased diversity? How might these responses inform educational policies and practices?

Of a total of 56 hours of observational data and 40 hours of interview data collected for the larger project, in Bonn Elementary School eight hours of observations and five hours of recorded interviews were conducted with the school administrator and two teachers. A local Mennonite pastor, a father of school-aged children, was also interviewed. He declined to be recorded, but field notes were taken during the interview. Data were analysed using the interactive model presented by Huberman and Miles (2001) in which collecting, analysing, and displaying data, and drawing and verifying tentative conclusions constitute a recursive process. The following section analyses excerpts from the interviews and field notes. Findings and discussion are grouped according to themes that emerged from the data with respect to supportive learning environments, inclusive pedagogies, proactive leadership, effective home–school collaboration, and challenges to EAL-inclusive pedagogy.

Findings and discussion

Supportive learning environments

The teachers interviewed for the current study were bilingual in Low and High German, the languages spoken by the newcomers at Bonn Elementary School. One teacher had the advantage of working in the school in multiple capacities over a 12-year period, initially as an educational assistant and, after gaining the relevant qualifications, returning as a full-time teacher. She commented on early attitudes towards lingusitic diversity as the school's demographic first began to change:

When I became an educational assistant back in 1997, I started out [working with pupils with][5] EAL. And at the time, what my administrator asked me to do was to never speak their language, and to me it didn't make any sense because I thought 'Well, I'm German', and it would only make them feel more relaxed in my presence if we spoke the same common language. Sometimes I'd slip up and start speaking German to them, and she would look at me sternly and say, 'We don't *do* that. We want to make sure they're immersed in English culture as much as possible.' So that was rather difficult for me because at the time I already had that philosophy. It didn't make sense first of all, and I thought I could bond better with them if we did speak the language.

(I: Teacher, 01/20/09: 2)

The attitudes and practices that characterized this teacher's early experiences indicate problematic assumptions about language learners that have been challenged by more critically oriented scholarship on language education. Cummins (2007), for example, points out that using pupils' first languages at school is not only important for forging social bonds, but that it is also instrumental in successful academic language learning. By the time the former educational assistant returned to Bonn Elementary School as a teacher, its learning environment had changed:

In about 2006 I rejoined the staff as a teacher. And at that point the philosophy was very much that you speak the pupil's native language and research had come [out supporting this approach]. That was right up my alley, what I had always believed in and kind of innately thought made sense, right? So that's been wonderful. And now I've got a bunch of EAL pupils and I can speak High German with them. One boy in my class joined the school only last week. He comes from Germany, so now I can speak High German and Low German. I love it. It feels comfortable.

(I: Teacher, 01/20/09: 2)

This welcoming environment, where multilingualism is seen as an asset, was highlighted again during observations in the school, in which multilingual signage and written communications to parents were noted (O: 01/20/09: 4). Further evidence that an inclusive learning environment was created is provided below ('Proactive leadership').

Inclusive pedagogies

Pedagogical efforts to respond to the needs of learners with EAL included using key visuals to clarify meaning for those who could not yet engage with written English; giving reading instructions to pupils; and using German in class. One teacher described her efforts as follows:

> I use pictures as much as I can, I read the instructions for pupils, and I try to translate it over to their language if they don't understand. For example, this new boy from Germany, I've just been saying my instructions in German as well as English. And it's kind of been fun for me, and then my other kids are getting a grasp of his language as well so we're building a community around languages, so that he doesn't feel like it's a bad thing that he speaks another language.
>
> (I: Teacher, 01/20/09: 4)

The teacher's speaking to her class in English as well as in German was inclusive for the new boy from Germany, but it also created an environment for other pupils to engage positively with German. This type of practice indicates a more critical pedagogy in which the monolingual norms prevalent in Canadian education systems are challenged (Cummins, 2003). In this instance the challenge comes both from the teacher and from monolingual pupils, who in more traditional classrooms would not be required or expected to use languages other than English.

Proactive leadership

Speaking about his own background, and his experience of growing up in a community similar to the one he was now teaching in, the principal commented on the insights this gave him in his role as a school leader:

> I grew up in [a rural area of Manitoba] where a lot of Low German[-speaking newcomers resided]. There was a lot of movement between Mexico, Bolivia and Paraguay to [my community] for employment and then back. That's exactly what we have here, and so my childhood experience up has been very useful. It's given me a lot of empathy and a lot of understanding [and] direction as to how we would move in helping this group feel a part of our school community.
>
> (I: School Principal, 01/20/09: 3)

Having teachers in the school who spoke the first language of some of its pupils was positively exploited by the principal as a means of welcoming immigrant families and of establishing meaningful communcation with them. The principal described the means by which he ensured that parents who did not read or write could still engage directly with the school: first, the relevant staff were made responsible for phoning parents at home to notify them (in Low German) of school events; secondly, those staff were always available to answer calls from German-speaking parents. Resources were also put in place to ensure that the school provided services, including healthcare, that were of value to families:

> I very consciously tried to have as many healthcare or community agencies that were directed towards helping this group to meet in [the school], and to provide facilities for that, so that [families] would see, you know they could come here and they could get [services]. Well, I wanted that to be here [to show] this is just part of school and the health system...and all of us want to help you.
>
> (I: School Administrator, 01/20/09: 3)

Effective home and school collaboration

One of the ways in which the school facilitated effective relationships with parents and families was by reinforcing the importance of maintaining their first language at home. One of the teachers who had experienced anxiety about speaking German in Canada when she was young expressed her gratitude as an adult for having maintained her German, and was able to offer encouragement to pupils:

> I said to one of them 'You have to speak German at home', because she doesn't want to speak German – 'Mom and Dad say you should speak German at home.' I said, 'You know, it's such a rich language, keep it up, right?' So I'm encouraging them to maintain that at home as well.
>
> (I: Teacher, 01/20/09: 4)

This teacher's comment ensured that a consistent message was being delivered both by parents and teachers. This validated the concerns of immigrant parents (Guo, 2006) and split the responsibility for promoting multilingualism between the home and the school. The teacher's ability to relate to the lives of the pupils was echoed in perspectives about parent/teacher communications. These were initiated by the teacher and not only on occasions where a pupil was experiencing difficulties. Because the teachers wanted to establish a positive rapport and an open channel of communication, connecting with parents was made a priority from the beginning of the school year. As one teacher explained:

One of our mandates for the year is to connect with the parents before the end of September. I generally sense that they're worried until I call them, and then some of the moms, you can almost hear a sigh of relief going, 'oh, I can talk to this lady.' Because I remember my mom being horrified [about having] phone calls with teachers, we were interpreters at a young age: 'Here's a phone call from so and so's teacher, can you help me?' So I sense there's kind of a family sense of relief: 'oh, we can talk to that lady if we have a problem.' And that's one of my joys because my heart is with these families. I was part of that culture because my mom found it so frustrating to be in an English culture, so I love being able to call home and say, 'hi, how's it going?' I can speak German and so that's wonderful.

(I: Teacher, 01/20/09: 6–7)

Challenges to EAL-inclusive pedagogy

Comparing her experiences with two quite different sets of pupils, a teacher highlighted one major challenge to EAL-inclusive pedagogy. One group had difficulty learning language and academic content, while the other seemed to struggle and the teacher suspected that they may have had learning difficulties. The funding and testing this teacher mentions refer to protocols for identifying and supporting learners with special needs. It would include standardized assessments delivered by specialists and follow-up programming and planning that would be in place for the entire duration of the pupil's time in public school. In the words of the teacher:

I've had kids that come into my room, and by the end of the year they're reading at grade level. And sometimes they've jumped three grades between the beginning of the year, or whenever they arrived, and the end of the year. And I know that kid will be just fine; I don't worry one bit about that child. But my most frustrating moments are when I realize [some] kids need to be in the system for four years before they can get funding. Because we can already tell within the first half [of the] year whether they're going to be successful... I worry about one boy who's been in the program or been in the school for two years, but will have [to wait another] two more years before he'll get tested. By then he'll be in grade 6. And he'll be superbly overwhelmed. And I'm not a fan of kids getting lost in the system.

(I: Teacher, 01/20/09: 3;11)

A further challenge to inclusive pedagogy was identified in the interview with the school's Mennonite pastor. He was positive about what the wider school division was doing to support the children's language learning, and generally felt that the children were learning English quickly, effectively, and with the support of caring and knowledgeable teachers (O: Pastor, 01/21/09: 2). Although the pastor acknowledged the potential for first language loss, mentioning that the children may use German less frequently in Manitoba, this aspect was downplayed by his decree that that was to be expected. Of greater concern, however, was the potential loss of Mennonite cultural and religious values in the government-funded school system. The pastor recounted how some parishioners' decisions to migrate to Canada were partly motivated by the apparent hostility the German school system and media showed towards their beliefs. According to the pastor, many members of his community found the early introduction of sexual education in schooling problematic, and when they attempted to voice their concerns, they were vilified by the media (O: Pastor, 01/21/09: 6).

Similarly incongruent values between this particular religious community and the mainstream provincial government-funded school system were apparent in the draft of a letter the pastor shared that was going to be signed by some parents and intended for the school division. In the letter, parents expressed concern about a magic show that had been performed at one school. The magician engaged the children with illusions and told them to believe in themselves, when the message the church conveyed was to believe in God (O: Pastor, 01/21/09: 8). The experiences of this religious community suggest that the histories, experiences, and priorities of parents and other stakeholders need to be considered in educational planning and programming (Guo, 2006), and that culturally and linguisitically diverse communities may be dealing with a myriad of complex issues including religious beliefs and issues of language and culture maintenance.

Conclusions and recommendations

Research for the present study found evidence of exemplary practices in Bonn Elementary School to facilitate welcoming learning environments, inclusive pedagogies, strong leadership, and meaningful interactions between the home and the school for learners with EAL and their families. These practices included intentionally cultivating an atmosphere where multilingualism was viewed as a strength; deliberately using the children's first languages in the classroom and advocating their continued use at home; strategically hiring staff who spoke the languages of the pupils and families in the community;

and ensuring appropriate outreach to parents to establish fruitful dialogue between school and home.

The findings reinforced research that demonstrates that connections and relationships with schools can be extremely important to newcomer pupils and their families (e.g. Guo, 2006). Having multilingual school staff who made cultural and linguistic liaisons transformed the experience of many immigrant families who had initially felt uncomfortable entering the physical environment of the school. Once parents knew they could access information and support in their home languages, a conduit for further engagement was created.

Nevertheless, Bonn Elementary School encountered certain challenges in implementing inclusive pedagogy. In particular, teachers reported difficulty in trying to meet the needs of learners with EAL who had begun to show the characteristics of learning difficulties; this was because of the school division and provincial approach of delaying testing such learners for learning disabilities to allow them time to learn language without the risk of pathologizing them. Further, a compelling finding with respect to religious diversity was noted in the interview with the pastor. In the case of one Mennonite church community in a region of Manitoba with a strong Mennonite presence overall, parents were less concerned about the potential for language loss than about the potential loss of cultural and religious values.

These findings suggest that, if educators are to be better equipped to recognize and respond to pupils as multifaceted indivudals with complex needs, more research that explores the intersection of diversities – for example, learners with both EAL and special needs – and the influence of religion in culturally and linguistically diverse communities is needed.

Notes

[1] Pseudonymns are used for all institutions, localities, and people mentioned in this chapter.

[2] Learners with EAL in Manitoba are allocated four years of special government funding to be used by school divisions and schools to develop and implement appropriate academic and language support. The numbers reported here refer to the pupils who fall within the four-year funding period. Actual numbers of learners with EAL would be higher since pupils continue to be learners with EAL once the additional funding ceases.

[3] Refers to the type of data collected (I=interview, O=observation); the participant, if applicable; the date of data collection; and the page number of the interview transcript or field note as appropriate.

[4] Actual numbers of immigrants in the Canadian teaching force are unknown as this data is not collected, so I refer here to data collected with respect to 'visible minorities' in the teaching profession, recognizing that some of these individuals are immigrants while others are Canadian-born. The term 'visible minorities' is placed in quotation marks as it has been deemed racist by the United Nations and the Canadian Council

on Race Relations; however, it is the term used by Statistics Canada (Ryan, Pollock, and Antonelli, 2009).

[5] Square brackets enclose text added editorially to make the meaning of the quote clear, for example when pronouns have been used.

Acknowledgements

The author gratefully acknowledges the funding provided by the Prairie Metropolis Centre for conducting the research presented in this chapter.

References

Bennett, C.I., McWhorter, L.M., and Kuykendall, J.A. (2006) 'Will I ever teach? Latino and African American students' perspectives on PRAXIS I'. *American Educational Research Journal*, 43 (3), 531–75.

Carrier, K.A. and Cohen, J.A. (2005) 'Hispanic individuals in their communities: An untapped resource for increasing the bilingual teacher population'. *Journal of Hispanic Higher Education*, 4 (1), 51–63.

Carter, T., Pandey, M., and Townsend, J. (2010) *The Manitoba Provincial Nominee Program: Attraction, integration, and retention of immigrants* (IRPP Study 10). Montréal: Institute for Research on Public Policy.

Creswell, J.W. and Plano Clark, V.L. (2007) *Designing and Conducting Mixed Methods Research*. Thousand Oaks, CA: Sage.

Cummins, J. (2003) 'Challenging the construction of difference as deficit: Where are identity, intellect, imagination, and power in the new regime of truth?' In Trifonas, P.P. (ed.) *Pedagogies of Difference: Rethinking education for social change*. New York/London: RoutledgeFalmer.

— (2007) 'Rethinking monolingual instructional strategies in multilingual classrooms'. *Canadian Journal of Applied Linguistics*, 10 (2), 221–40.

Darder, A., Baltodano, M.P., and Torres, R.D. (eds) (2009) *The Critical Pedagogy Reader,* 2nd ed. New York: Routledge.

Failler, A. (2009) 'Racial grief and melancholic agency'. In Campbell, S., Meynell, L., and Sherwin, S. (eds) *Embodiment and Agency*. University Park, PA: Penn State University Press.

Furman, J.S. (2008) 'Tensions in multicultural teacher education research: Demographics and the need to demonstrate effectiveness'. *Education and Urban Society*, 41 (1), 55–79.

Giroux, H. and Giroux, S.S. (2008) 'Challenging neoliberalism's new world order: The promise of critical pedagogy'. In Denzin, N.K., Lincoln, Y.S., and Smith, L.T. (eds) *Handbook of Critical and Indigenous Methodologies*. Thousand Oaks, CA: Sage.

Guo, Y. (2006) 'Why didn't they show up? Rethinking ESL parent involvement in K-12 education'. *TESL Canada Journal*, 24 (1), 80–95.

Huberman, A.M., and Miles, M.B. (2001) 'Data management and analysis methods'. In Conrad, C.F., Haworth, J.G., and Lattuca, L.R. (eds) *Qualitative Research in Higher Education: Expanding perspectives*. New York, NY: Pearson.

Kearney, J.E. (2008) 'Factors affecting satisfaction and retention of African American and European American teachers in an urban school district: Implications for building and maintaining teachers employed in school districts across the nation'. *Education and Urban Society*, 40 (5), 613–27.

Lotherington, H. (2007) 'Rewriting traditional tales as multilingual narratives at elementary school: Problems and progress'. *Canadian Journal of Applied Linguistics*, 10 (2), 241–55.

Manitoba Education, Citizenship and Youth (2006) *Belonging, Learning, Growing: Kindergarten to Grade 12 Action Plan for Ethnocultural Equity*. Winnipeg, MB: MECY.

Nieto, S. (2010) 'Language, diversity, and learning: Lessons for education in the 21st century'. *Center for Applied Linguistics Digest*, August, 1–4.

Quiocho, A. and Rios, F. (2000) 'The power of their presence: Minority group teachers and schooling'. *Review of Educational Research*, 70 (4), 485–528.

Reitz, J. (2011) *Pro-immigration Canada: Social and economic roots of popular views* (IRPP Study 20). Montréal: Institute for Research on Public Policy.

Ryan, J., Pollock, K., and Antonelli, F. (2009) 'Teacher diversity in Canada: Leaky pipelines, bottlenecks, and glass ceilings'. *Canadian Journal of Education*, 32 (3), 591–617.

Schmidt, C. (2005) 'From teacher candidates to ESL ambassadors in teacher education'. In *TESL-EJ*, 9 (2), 1–11.

— (2010) 'Systemic discrimination as a barrier for immigrant teachers'. *Diaspora, Indigenous, and Minority Education*, 4 (4), 235–52.

— (2011) 'Multilingualism in Canadian schools: Current issues and perspectives'. In Neumann, U. and Schneider, J. (eds) *Schools with Migrant Students: Viewing diversity as resource*. Münster: WaxmannVerlag.

Schmidt, C. and Block, L. (2010) 'Without and within: The implications of employment and ethnocultural equity policies for internationally educated teachers'. *Canadian Journal of Educational Administration and Policy*, 100.

Schmidt, C., Schellenberg, V., and Turner, D. (2009) 'Teaching and diversity: Education, immigration, and multiculturalism'. Workshop delivered at the 11th National Metropolis Conference. Calgary AB, March 19–22.

Schmidt, C., Young, J., and Mandzuk, D. (2010) 'The integration of immigrant teachers in Manitoba, Canada: Critical issues and perspectives'. *Journal of International Migration and Integration*, 11 (4), 1–14.

Solomon, R.P., Portelli, J.P., Daniel, B., and Campbell, A. (2005) 'The discourse of denial: How white teacher candidates construct race, racism and "white privilege"'. *Race, Ethnicity, and Education*, 8 (2), 147–69.

Tatar, M. and Horenczyk, G. (2003) 'Diversity-related burnout amongst teachers'. *Teaching and Teacher Education*, 19, 397–408.

Chapter 5

The development of a collaborative school culture: The case of an inner-city school in Reykjavík, Iceland

Hanna Ragnarsdóttir and Börkur Hansen

This chapter illuminates how leadership, pedagogy, and home–school collaboration at a school in Iceland can actively build on diversity. It also sheds light on the development of a school culture where diversity is seen as a valuable feature.

Although migration has taken place since time immemorial (Castles and Miller, 2009), the distinctive features of migration in recent years are its global scope, its centrality to domestic and international politics, and the enormous economic and social consequences that it has had. In times of extensive migration and globalization, the diverse experiences, knowledge, cultures, languages, and religions of teachers are important for equally diverse school communities. School principals worldwide are being confronted with the task of leading schools whose pupils are, in terms of culture and language, increasingly diverse (Lumby and Coleman, 2007; Ryan, 2003). Teachers with equally diverse backgrounds are important as role models for these pupils (Bartolo and Smyth, 2009). Iceland is just one country where this challenge applies. As immigration to Iceland has increased in recent years, its schools have become ever more diverse in terms of the languages, cultures, and religions both of their pupils and of their teachers.

In this chapter, that reality is illustrated by the case study of an inner-city school in Reykjavík for pupils aged 6 to 16. The school is one of many where ethnic, linguistic, and religious diversity has been regarded as positive for pupils and staff, and is seen as bringing new dimensions and dynamics to the school's culture.

The school has what Hargreaves (2003) describes as a 'collaborative culture'. The staff share the values of cooperation and develop and implement a rich learning environment for all pupils, whatever their language, race, or ethnicity.

The conceptual and theoretical context

Leadership and school cultures in diverse schools

In many countries, the growing diversity in their schools has been the focus of considerable scholarship in recent decades, raising such questions as the extent to which schools should adjust to this new reality. The effects of diverse cultural and religious values on the development of school cultures, how equality in school communities may be attained, and how the marginalization of minority groups may be avoided are all relevant areas for research (Hansen and Ragnarsdóttir, 2010). Scholars have focused on the situation in countries where most teachers belong to a cultural majority while the pupils are diverse in terms of cultures, languages, and religions. Thus there is a mismatch between the diversity of pupils and the homogeneity of teachers (Ladson-Billings, 2001; Lumby and Coleman, 2007; Schmidt and Block, 2010), which forces us to consider what challenges this might create. According to Schmidt and Block (*ibid.*), children can experience exclusion if they do not have the chance to see themselves reflected in their school surroundings and cannot identify with them.

Many scholars claim that schools where the teachers form a homogeneous group do not have the benefit of the experiences, strengths, and insights of a culturally and religiously diverse group of teachers (e.g. Bartolo and Smyth, 2009; Santoro, 2007; Schmidt and Block, 2010). Vertovec (2009) observes that transnational experiences provide particular knowledge, and enable people to become active participants in different cultures and across national borders. What Vertovec identifies as 'transnational competence' is likely to be found among ethnically diverse teachers, and it is an important resource for diverse learners at a time when communication across cultures is manifold.

Texts on the subject of diverse teachers and learners have focused mainly on equality, participation, and barriers to participation. The issues that they debate include equal rights of participation, equal access, and opportunities for teachers and pupils (Banks, 2007; Gundara, 2000; Nieto, 2010). Authors have also considered how to remove obstacles to inclusion by developing new visions and structures for school communities (Ragnarsdóttir, 2008; Santoro, 2007; Schmidt and Block, 2010).

Leadership is an important factor in restructuring school communities and developing inclusive school cultures. Hargreaves (2003) observes that school cultures can be characterized in ways that range from 'fragmented individualism' to 'collaboration' – they can be anywhere on a spectrum that emphasizes individual efforts at one end and collaboration between teachers at the other. To achieve the desired collaborative culture, Hargreaves and Fink (2006) claim that all change and development have to be sustainable in order to preserve the arrangements that enhance learning. To create stability and progress, school leadership has to include 'depth, length, breadth, justice, diversity, resourcefulness, and conservation' (*ibid.*: 18).

Parekh (2006) states that each multicultural society must find its own balance and achieve equal opportunities and equal access by ensuring that groups and individuals actively communicate and reach points of agreement without losing their coherence. Similar challenges confront schools in multicultural societies. Critical pedagogy is a useful approach: it stresses such concepts as voice, dialogue, equality, empowerment, and social justice (Cummins, 2003; Freire, 2005; Giroux, 2009), and presupposes that knowledge is never neutral and that schooling always presumes certain social, historical, and political circumstances.

Cummins (2003) maintains that, in the history of almost every country, the majority – i.e. the ruling groups – have systematically organized education around majority values, so that differences in background, gender, social class, and language are seen as a deficit. Nieto (2010) argues that, when young people enter schools, they are entering institutions that have already made fundamental decisions about what is worth knowing and what it means to be educated. As a result, some of these children may be excluded through no fault of their own. A so-called deficit perspective, which emphasizes the disadvantage and inferiority of certain groups and individuals based on gender, race, class, and ethnicity (Gundara, 2000; Nieto, 2010) thereby becomes the explanation for their failure because the inequity embedded in educational structures remains unhighlighted.

Cummins (2003) discusses how a society's rulers affect the definition of teachers' roles – such as their mindset, aspirations, and attitudes – and the organization of education – such as the curriculum, evaluation, and languages used in teaching. He maintains that one of the problems in schools is that the value of pupils' cultures, languages, identities, and intellect is overlooked, while their perceived deficits are emphasized. Cummins argues that schools must not only acknowledge the cultural wealth that pupils bring with them, but that they must also build on this wealth when developing curricula for teaching and teacher education.

Nieto (2010) notes that, while immigrant pupils need to adapt to their new country's schools and learn the majority language, schools also need to negate inequalities that arise when, for example, the pupils' languages or dialects are treated disrespectfully. According to Nieto, schools must ensure that pupils' languages are valued and used in the classroom.

The act of teaching can also perpetuate inequalities. If teaching builds primarily on the experiences and knowledge of the majority pupils, pupils from minority groups may be unable to identify with them. Gay (2000) and Ladson-Billings (1994) both argue that teaching should build on the knowledge and experiences that each pupil brings. In Iceland research findings have indicated that their command of Icelandic is the criterion by which pupils from minority backgrounds are evaluated, while their diverse experiences and knowledge are ignored. These findings confirm that a deficit model is being used in schools (Ragnarsdóttir, 2008). Many studies have indicated that a pupil's knowledge in his or her own mother tongue is not considered an asset or strength if that mother tongue is not the majority language (Bhatti, 1999; Brooker, 2002; Nieto, 2010).

The Icelandic background and context

Immigrants in Iceland

The languages, cultures, and religions of Iceland's population have become increasingly diverse in recent decades. In 1995, the proportion of non-Icelandic citizens was 1.8 per cent of the total population. In 2000, it was 2.6 per cent; in 2005, 3.6 per cent; and in 2011, 6.6 per cent (Hagstofa Íslands [Statistics Iceland], 2011a).

Pupils

In 2010, out of a total of 42,539 pupils in Iceland's compulsory schools, those whose mother tongue was not Icelandic was 2,318 (5.4 per cent). Between them, these pupils had 43 different mother tongues, though the number could be higher since the mother tongue of 38 of the pupils was not specified (Hagstofa Íslands [Statistics Iceland], 2011b).

In the same year, of the 18,961 children in Iceland's preschools, the number with a mother tongue other than Icelandic was 1,815 (9.5 per cent) These children had 41 different mother tongues, with numbers varying greatly between schools (*ibid.*).

Teachers

Information on teachers' backgrounds is not officially registered in Iceland, so that a reliable picture of teachers' mother tongues and ethnicities is not easy to obtain. However, teachers' age, gender, education, and country of origin are well documented. A detailed study conducted in 2005–06 (Lassen,

2007) detected 84 foreign-born teachers in Icelandic compulsory schools. These teachers, who constituted 2 per cent of Iceland's teacher population, originated from 29 different countries in all continents.

According to research, an indefinite number of internationally educated teachers in Iceland are employed in areas other than teaching. One ongoing study shows that the majority of the 20 qualified Polish teachers employed to teach at a Polish school on Saturdays are not working as teachers elsewhere during the rest of the week (Zielińska *et al.*, in press; Szkoła Polska w Reykjaviku, 2010). Similarly, findings from a recent survey among immigrants indicate that 50 per cent of those who are employed have jobs where their education is neither relevant nor applied. The same survey revealed that 74 per cent of immigrants have not tried to have their education accredited (Félagsvísindastofnun HÍ [Social Science Research Institute, University of Iceland] and Fjölmenningarsetur [Multicultural and Information Centre], 2009).

On the other hand, although their numbers are unknown there are more internationally educated teachers and assistants working in preschools than in compulsory schools in Iceland (Ragnarsdóttir, 2010).

The Ministry of Education, Science and Culture (Mennta- og menningarmálaráðuneytið, 2011) certifies people to work as preschool teachers, compulsory school teachers, and upper secondary school teachers, but neither it nor Iceland's universities provide orientation for internationally educated teachers. However, a number of immigrants with a university education are registered in teacher training programmes at the University of Iceland (Háskóli Íslands, 2010).

Equality and participation – and the obstacles

The legislation governing pre-, compulsory, and upper secondary schools in Iceland (Lög um framhaldsskóla [Upper Secondary School Act] no. 92/2008; Lög um grunnskóla [Compulsory School Act] no. 91/2008; Lög um leikskóla [Preschool Act] no. 90/2008) is based on principles of equality. These laws stipulate that schools should benefit all pupils and educate each child effectively.

Although the issue of diversity is not specifically addressed in this legislation in the way it has been internationally (see, for example, OECD, 2010 and UNESCO, 2010), particular sections of the acts deal with pupils with special needs and with languages other than Icelandic. The OECD report, *Educating Teachers for Diversity: Meeting the challenge* (OECD, 2010) states that a pupil's background, whether culturally or economically different from the so-called majority, has a profound impact on their achievement. The report goes on to stress that education systems should ensure that all pupils have equal access to studies and that diversity among pupils and teachers is a resource. Findings from recent research in Iceland indicate that pupils from ethnic minority backgrounds encounter obstacles in educational access and participation, including pedagogy, evaluation methods, and materials (Ragnarsdóttir, 2008; Ragnarsdóttir and Loftsdóttir, 2010). Similarly, teachers from ethnic minority backgrounds have experienced marginalization and exclusion (Ragnarsdóttir, 2010; Ragnarsdóttir and Blöndal, 2007, 2010).

Method

The case study of the Reykjavík school that forms the subject of this chapter was conducted in 2010–11. This specific case is analysed from different angles (Cohen *et al.*, 2000), with the aim of providing a precise description or reconstruction (Flick, 2006). The school was chosen for the diversity of its teachers and pupils. It has also served as a model school for multicultural education and has formed part of a development project on the same theme.

Data collection included semi-structured interviews with the principal and four teachers, all of whom were leaders in culturally responsive pedagogies. A focus group interview was also conducted with three ethnic minority teachers. According to Flick (2006), group discussions correspond to the way in which opinions are formed, expressed, and exchanged in everyday life. Each interview lasted between 60 and 90 minutes and was transcribed, coded, and categorized (*ibid.*; Kvale, 1996).

Documents analysed included the school policy, the curriculum guide, and an evaluation report from the Reykjavík Educational Central Office (Menntasvið Reykjavíkur, 2010), as well as reports on standardized tests and the school's Programme for International Student Assessment (PISA) surveys. The case study also draws on findings from interviews with 27 of the school's current and former pupils from ethnic minorities.

Findings

The inner-city school: history, policy, and vision

Opened in 1930, the school is one of the oldest compulsory schools in Reykjavík, located near the city centre. The school's first principal was a well-known educational leader while many of the 32 teachers also there at the start were also notable writers and poets. The school building, which was considered modern at the time, included 30 classrooms, special rooms for science, art, handicrafts, and home economics, a swimming pool, and a gym. This structure called for new, more flexible pedagogies and the abolition of traditional formalities. For example, the children were allowed to enter the school as soon as they arrived, instead of queuing up outside and filing in together. In about 1950, pupil numbers reached a peak, with 1,839 schoolchildren. Now there are 479 pupils aged 6 to 16 and a staff of 79. The policy of the school is based on legislation and international agreements, as well as the educational policy of Reykjavík (Lög um grunnskóla [Compulsory School Act] no. 91/2008; Reykjavíkurborg [City of Reykjavík], 2011a).

The school is multicultural: 20 per cent of the pupils have a foreign background and represent 30 different nationalities. It has the highest number of pupils receiving funding for instruction in Icelandic as a second language in Reykjavík (Reykjavíkurborg [City of Reykjavík], 2011a). In 2011, 82 of its pupils received such funding.

The school is inclusive, with teaching adapted to each pupil's needs. Based on observations of 25 classes, an evaluation report from the Reykjavík Educational Central Office (Menntasvið Reykjavíkur [Reykjavík Educational Central Office], 2010) identified high-quality teaching, active pupils, and effective classroom management. Furthermore, the school has adapted and developed a programme for collaborative teaching to encourage all pupils to participate.

Findings from a study of 27 current and former ethnic minority pupils support this evaluation. They reveal that the pupils – who came to Iceland from various countries in Africa, Asia, South America, and Europe between 2003 and 2008 – were satisfied with their time at the school. The pupils mentioned that they had supportive teachers and high-quality teaching, and that they made academic progress (Magnúsdóttir, 2010).

For many years the school has been a model for multicultural education in Reykjavík (Menntasvið Reykjavíkur [Reykjavík Educational Central Office], 2010). Its recognition of the inherent diversity of people according to their gender, family situation, values, religion, interests, and abilities is reflected in all its teaching. According to its website, the school adheres to the philosophy of multicultural education, which affects child development and originated in Europe in the 1970s. Until that time the main emphasis in many European countries had been on so-called educational programmes for immigrants, a policy designed to assimilate them into the host society and obliterate all aspects of their native culture, including their language.

Assimilation as an educational response to diversity is further explored by Chris Gaine (2005), who claims that assimilation was 'a perspective focusing on minorities as immigrants with incompatible and probably inferior cultures; the educational focus was upon conformity and reducing difference, making the strangers less strange' (*ibid.*: 29). According to Gaine, it was in the 1970s and 1980s that multiculturalism developed as an educational response to diversity. It sought to 'celebrate diversity rather than eliminate it, aiming to emphasise respect and mutual understanding, making the strangers less strange to "us"' (*ibid.*).

As stated on the school's website, the aim of multicultural education is for pupils to learn to respect diversity and build on it in a positive manner. To achieve this objective, the school is developing pedagogies to teach collaboration, mutual respect, and the value of diversity. Teachers are encouraged to utilize diverse pedagogies so that pupils may actively participate in classes and build on their abilities.

Leadership and school culture

The principal has worked at the school for 38 years, first as a teacher, and as principal since 1995. He has a positive view of diversity – describing diverse pupils and teachers as resources – and sees the only challenge in employing diverse teachers and leading a diverse school as being to ensure an atmosphere of respect and wellbeing. He emphasizes the importance of building on the strengths and abilities of everyone and creating a culture of collaboration.

The teachers and assistants from ethnic minority backgrounds demonstrate a range of fluency in Icelandic. Although some have university degrees, according to the principal the only positions available to those without proficiency in Icelandic are as assistants, since teaching in an Icelandic compulsory school requires fluency in the language. However, some employees who started as assistants and became familiar with teaching did go on to become teachers, though others left for better-paid jobs. The principal says that many in his workforce have learnt Icelandic quickly simply by conversing with colleagues and pupils. He notes how fortunate he has been to employ teachers and assistants who speak a range of languages, since this has significantly aided in communication with minority children and their families (Bartolo and Smyth, 2009).

Following some racist incidents in the school in 1999, prolonged discussions among the principal, teachers, and pupils resulted in the establishment of a policy of mutual respect. This in turn led to an anti-discriminatory project, which was launched in 2001. It was supported by the municipality and for the five years that it ran a Belgian expert was on hand to offer advice.

According to the principal, the project was grounded in diversity – a natural move for a school where ethnic diversity was a recent development, but where pupils had been diverse in terms of social class since the 1930s. Although the school terminated the project to save money, it continues to build on the gains that the project brought during the time that it ran. The principal is aware of the importance of leading continued discussions among teachers on issues of diversity and equality.

The school currently employs two ethnic minority teachers and four assistants. The findings of a focus group interview with two of the teachers and one assistant highlight their view of the school as a natural home for multicultural education and multicultural policy. These staff members see the inclusive approach of multicultural education as recognizing and respecting diversity. Not only is multiculturalism the stated policy: it is reflected in everyday practices in the school.

The 2010 evaluation report (Menntasvið Reykjavíkur [Reykjavík Educational Central Office], 2010) states that patience and tolerance characterize the school staff. While the social conditions of many pupils are extremely difficult, the school scores highly on pupils' level of wellbeing and provides flexible support to all pupils according to their needs. The teachers and assistants likewise find that the school's multicultural approach makes them feel welcome; they feel that they belong to the school community and that their voices are heard. They talk about everyone's democratic participation in the school's development and decision-making – an aspect confirmed by the high scores on leadership and collaboration of the principal and the assistant principal in the 2010 evaluation report. The report states that there is general satisfaction with their leadership style; that both are accessible and helpful, with good communication skills; that their relations with staff are based on trust and respect; and that both are flexible and open to change.

The teachers and assistants regard it as essential that diversity among pupils is reflected in the staff. They see the staff's diversity as including different ethnic and linguistic groups, both genders, a range of ages, and a variety of interests, noting that such variety means that the workplace is never boring, and that lively debates are common. They also refer to the opportunities that the school provides for ethnic minorities – for example, by offering space for meetings between different ethnic groups. The report reiterates that the school has a strong culture based on values of understanding, flexibility, and respect for diversity.

The same report highlights the fact that the school scores above the national average in all standardized test results (Menntasvið Reykjavíkur [Reykjavík Educational Central Office], 2010). An unofficial report from the Educational Testing Institute of Iceland (Námsmatsstofnun, 2011), meanwhile, suggests that the 2009 results from the OECD Programme for International Student Assessment (PISA) were equally high. Furthermore, according to several external and internal surveys, pupils' level of wellbeing in the school is above the national average. In these surveys, wellbeing refers primarily to satisfaction with the school and self-efficacy, as well as the freedom from bullying and anxiety.

Religions

The diverse religious backgrounds of pupils and staff at the school encompass Christianity, Islam, Buddhism, and Hinduism. According to the principal, discussions among teachers about different religions have taken place in the school for many years. A group of 12 religious studies teachers and assistants was formed five years ago to discuss religious matters in teaching and other related practices within the school. According to the school's website, the group has been supervised by diverse religious leaders for the past three years, though informal discussions on religious matters had taken place for some considerable time before this. The principal notes, for example, that the school has reached an agreement to visit a church before Christmas.

The discussion group has recommended that the school respond to the growing pupil diversity by teaching about religions in all classes and at all levels so as to counteract misunderstanding, conflict, and prejudice. Teaching about religions is seen as a way of increasing awareness and understanding of different cultures and societies, and it can be easily linked to other subjects in the curriculum. On the basis of the group's recommendations, the school recently established its imperatives of policy, demonstrating leadership on the issue.

In October 2011, a little later, the city council passed equivalent policies regarding collaboration between preschools, compulsory schools, and the Department of Recreational Activities developed by Reykjavík's municipality and religious denominations. They support open discussions within schools about religions, in which teachers emphasize the equity of religious views (Reykjavíkurborg [City of Reykjavík], 2011b).

Home–school collaboration

The school welcomes all new pupils and their families to meetings where certain people are present: a supervisory teacher, teachers of Icelandic as a second language and, if needed, an interpreter. As well as biannual meetings with pupils and parents, the school has invited parents to information sessions where they can communicate via the internal web, for example. Participation in new information sessions for parents has generally been good and the parents' association has encouraged ethnic minority parents to take part.

The school has additional ways of reaching out to ethnic minority parents, including special meetings and formal and informal discussions between principals, teachers, and parents. According to the 2010 evaluation report (Menntasvið Reykjavíkur [Reykjavík Educational Central Office], 2010), the principal and the head of the parents' association collaborate closely. Teachers in the school emphasize the importance of initiating contact with parents since collaboration impacts particularly on the wellbeing and progress of the immigrant children.

According to the teachers, all the parents are generally concerned that every pupil and their family participate in the school community. Aware that many speak different languages, the school has taken the following measures so as to avoid misunderstanding and exclusion: the parents ensure that all families receive messages related to after-school gatherings and the social activities of particular classes; if necessary, interpreters are used in dialogues with ethnic minority parents; written communications are translated into the home languages of the families where necessary; and school policy is available on the website in six languages besides Icelandic. Furthermore, information on various matters – such as parent–teacher meetings, attitude surveys, and summer vacations – is available in ten different languages from the Reykjavík Educational Central Office website (Reykjavíkurborg [City of Reykjavík], 2011c).

Pedagogy

The school website contains references to a programme called CLIM (Cooperative Learning in Multicultural Groups), which was initiated at the time of the Multicultural Education Development Programme (Paelman, 2001). The website states that all schools are charged with preparing their pupils for life in a multicultural society. By focusing on diversity, which consists not only of differences but also of similarities, intercultural education is a way of meeting this need. CLIM makes optimal use of this diversity to stimulate each pupil to learn. In CLIM, teachers organize groups of pupils with different abilities, problem-solving strategies, and experiences, and allocate roles to each pupil. The teachers delegate authority to the pupils, who collaborate in setting norms for their group and working on their tasks. Pupils' roles vary in a systematic way, from one task to another, so that each one experiences all the different roles and responsibilities. At the same time, the teacher's role changes from that of leader to that of supervisor and observer.

CLIM is based on 'Complex Instruction' (CI), a type of cooperative learning. Its main aims are to 'get every pupil to learn', and to increase the level of conceptual thinking. CI was developed by Elizabeth Cohen (1994) at Stanford University and brought to Europe by a European project: CLIM. In CI pupils are required to deal with diversity within their group – and thus to apply intercultural skills. The benefit of CLIM is that it combines intercultural learning with conceptual thinking.

According to the teachers interviewed in the school, CLIM has made a significant contribution to the school's collaborative atmosphere, although some teachers use it more than others. The principles of CLIM make it more suitable to certain subjects than to others.

THE STORY OF THOR – THE MUSIC TEACHER

Thor has been a music teacher at the school for some years. He has been very active in curriculum development, both within the school and at national level. He has published music books and developed materials on music teaching in compulsory schools.

Thor says that a few years ago he took a period of leave and went to university in Denmark to study conducting and music teaching. When he returned, approaches to teaching were being changed so as to meet the needs of the increasing ethnic diversity in the school's pupil population. He says that the CLIM method was being implemented with the leadership of one of his fellow teachers and the support of the Reykjavík Educational Central Office.

In an interview about his teaching he said that he would need to utilize his music background constructively in this new context: 'the main task is to involve all the pupils', and to make sure that they have 'specific roles in the groups I create for them', irrespective of their ethnicity. He says that it is of central importance 'that they are all involved in playing the music that they choose'. According to Thor, they can all 'make a contribution' by playing the diverse range of instruments that he has access to in his classroom. His task is to influence the pupils so that every one of them feels that they can participate.

Thor says that, when an immigrant pupil – from China, for example – joins his class, he does not automatically introduce Chinese music to the class. Instead, he creates a role for that pupil in the group: 'I place him in a group to play an instrument that I sense he can play without much difficulty.' The music selected or created varies according to the capacity of the children. So being from China or wherever the pupil comes from is not, in Thor's view, the issue. Rather, 'the issue is to create conditions for cooperation by having fun playing the music with a variety of instruments'. He also changes roles within and across the groups he establishes in line with the CLIM method 'in order to prevent the best musicians from controlling the situation too much' so that all the pupils have a chance to experiment with different instruments.

To Thor, this approach is a good way to reach all children by 'using music as the language of communication' instead of using 'spoken language'. For him, the teaching task is not to create a situation of competition between pupils about who is the best player. Rather, it is to involve everyone at their own level. He says that this should be emphasized in sport and other curricular activities as well, because 'otherwise we create winners and losers', whereas 'our task is to make sure that we have as many winners as possible'. He maintains that 'we should not forget that folk music in places like Africa and Cuba did not divide people into players and listeners – all involved were active participants'.

Thor is also very keen on involving people in his environment to add flavour to his music teaching, such as parents who play specific instruments, African groups he is in contact with, and so forth. His main task is to create a sense of fun and enjoyment that relies on cooperation, respect, and tolerance for the other party. 'This is my version of the CLIM method,' concludes Thor.

Two of Thor's former pupils (brothers of African origin) now play in a popular band in Iceland, and have performed in many countries and have international contracts. In a recent newspaper interview, their mother describes how Thor encouraged the boys and supported their musical talents. She believes that the school's environment and ethos, the diversity of its pupils, and the high quality of the music teaching in the school were instrumental in her sons' development as successful musicians. When asked why she stayed in Iceland, she replied that her sons would have liked to move to her country of origin, 'but only if they could take their school with them' (Fréttablaðið, 2012).

Conclusion

The CLIM method established a value base that has become a distinct feature in the school's culture. The value base emphasizes individualized teaching pedagogies and the inclusion of pupils. The school leaders and the staff are all committed to this value base (Menntasvið Reykjavíkur [Reykjavík Educational Central Office], 2010). Staff collaboration and the strategic bringing together of parents and experts are distinctive features of the school's culture.

Collaboration on multicultural issues is essential in creating a school environment where diversity is seen as a valuable feature (Nieto, 2010; Ryan, 2003). Within a collaborative school culture, all pupils and staff have a say in creating a rich learning environment where diversity is respected and valued (Gay, 2000; Nieto, 2010). All their voices are heard and efforts are made to encourage everyone to participate. Issues of equity and social justice are the guiding principles (Gundara, 2000), and this school has managed to a large extent to follow these principles. Many aspects of the school, such as its organization, leadership, teaching, and home–school collaboration bear witness to an educational setting that openly values diversity. Its history of innovative practices supports its recent development as a leading school in multicultural education in Reykjavík. Hargreaves and Fink (2006) point out that maintaining an effective learning environment is a difficult task. The challenge for the inner-city school discussed in this chapter will therefore be to sustain its collaborative culture.

Acknowledgements
This study was funded by the University of Iceland Research Fund and the School of Education, University of Iceland.

References
Banks, J.A. (2007) 'Multicultural education: Characteristics and goals'. In Banks, J.A. and Banks, C.A.M. (eds) *Multicultural Education: Issues and perspectives*, 3rd ed. New York: John Wiley and Sons.

Bartolo, P. and Smyth, G. (2009) 'Teacher education for diversity'. In Swennen, A. and van der Klink, M. (eds) *Becoming a Teacher Educator: Theory and practice for teacher educators*. Amsterdam: Springer.

Bhatti, G. (1999) *Asian Children at Home and at School: An ethnographic study*. London: Routledge.

Brooker, L. (2002) *Starting School: Young children learning cultures*. Buckingham: Open University Press.

Castles, S. and Miller, M.J. (2009) *The Age of Migration: International population movements in the modern world*, 4th ed. New York: Guilford.

Cohen, E.G. (1994) *Designing Groupwork: Strategies for the heterogeneous classroom*, 2nd ed. New York: Teachers College Press.

Cohen, L., Manion, L., and Morrison, K. (2000) *Research Methods in Education*, 5th ed. London: RoutledgeFalmer.

Cummins, J. (2003) 'Challenging the construction of difference as deficit: Where are identity, intellect, imagination, and power in the new regime of truth?' In Trifonas, P.P. (ed.) *Pedagogies of Difference: Rethinking education for social change*. New York: RoutledgeFalmer.

Félagsvísindastofnun HÍ [Social Science Research Institute, University of Iceland] and Fjölmenningarsetur [Multicultural and Information Centre] (2009) Innflytjendur á Íslandi. Viðhorfskönnun. Online. www.fel.hi.is/sites/files/fel/Innflytjendur_skyrsla.pdf (accessed 27 September 2011).

Flick, U. (2006) *An Introduction to Qualitative Research*, 3rd ed. London: Sage.

Freire, P. (2005) *Education for Critical Consciousness*. London: Continuum.

Fréttablaðið (2012) Synirnir eru bestu vinir mínir/My sons are my best friends. Online. www.visir.is/synirnir-eru-bestu-vinir-minir/article/2012702189973 (accessed 23 May 2012).

Gaine, C. (2005) *We're All White, Thanks: The persisting myth about 'white' schools*. Stoke on Trent: Trentham.

Gay, G. (2000) *Culturally Responsive Teaching: Theory, research and practice*. New York: Teachers College Press.

Giroux, H.A. (2009) 'Critical theory and educational practice'. In Darder, A,, Baltodano, M.P., and Torres, R.D. (eds) *The Critical Pedagogy Reader*, 2nd ed. New York: Routledge.

Gundara, J.S. (2000) *Interculturalism, Education and Inclusion*. London: Paul Chapman.

Hagstofa Íslands [Statistics Iceland] (2011a) 'Population by Origin and Citizenship'. Online: www.statice.is/Statistics/Population/Citizenship-and-country-of-birth (accessed 25 October 2011).

— (2011b) 'Education'. Online. www.statice.is/Statistics/Education (accessed 27 October 2011).

Hansen, B. and Ragnarsdóttir, H. (2010) Fjölmenning og þróun skóla. In Ragnarsdóttir, H. and Jónsdóttir, E.S. (eds) *Fjölmenning og skólastarf*. Reykjavík: Rannsóknastofa í fjölmenningarfræðum and Háskólaútgáfan.

Hargreaves, A. (2003) *Changing Teachers, Changing Times: Teachers' work and culture in the postmodern age*. New York: Teachers College Press.

Hargreaves, A. and Fink, D. (2006) *Sustainable Leadership*. San Francisco: Jossey-Bass.

Háskóli Íslands [University of Iceland] (2010) Teaching studies, diploma programme. Online. https://ugla.hi.is/kennsluskra/index.php?tab=skoli&chapter=content&id=17578&kennsluar=2010 (accessed 27 September 2011).

Kvale, S. (1996) *Interviews: An introduction to qualitative research interviewing*. Thousand Oaks: Sage.

Ladson-Billings, G. (1994) *The Dreamkeepers: Successful teachers of African American children*. San Francisco: Jossey-Bass.

— (2001) *Crossing Over to Canaan: The journey of new teachers in diverse classrooms*. San Francisco: Jossey-Bass.

Lassen, B.H. (2007)' Í tveimur menningarheimum: reynsla og upplifun kennara af erlendum uppruna af því að starfa í grunnskólum á Íslandi'. Unpublished MEd thesis, Iceland University of Education, Reykjavík.

Lumby, J. and Coleman, M. (2007) *Leadership and Diversity: Challenging theory and practice in education*. London: Sage.

Lög um framhaldsskóla [Upper Secondary School Act] no. 92/2008.

Lög um grunnskóla [Compulsory School Act] no. 91/2008.

Lög um leikskóla [Preschool Act] no. 90/2008.

Magnúsdóttir, N.V. (2010) 'Allir vilja eignast íslenskar vinir. Hverjar eru helstu hindranir á vegi erlendra grunn- og framhaldsskólanemenda í íslensku skólakerfi?' Unpublished MEd thesis, University of Iceland, Reykjavík,

Mennta- og menningarmálaráðuneytið [Ministry of Education, Science and Culture] (2011) Licence Application. Online. http://eng.menntamalaraduneyti.is/licence/ (accessed 27 September 2011).

Menntasvið Reykjavíkur [Reykjavík Educational Central Office] (2010) (The inner city school) – heildarmat á skólastarfi. Online. www.austurbaejarskoli.is/pdf/mat/heildarmat10.pdf (accessed 27 September 2011).

Námsmatsstofnun [Educational Testing Institute of Iceland] (2011) 'Niðurstöður PISA 2009 rannsóknarinnar'. Online. www.namsmat.is/vefur/rannsoknir/pisa_kynning2009.html (accessed 27 September 2011).

Nieto, S. (2010) *The Light in Their Eyes: Creating multicultural learning communities*, 10th anniversary ed. New York: Teachers College Press.

OECD. Centre for Educational Research and Innovation (CERI) (2010) 'Educating teachers for diversity: Meeting the challenge'. Online. www.oecd.org/documen t/38/0,3343,en_2649_35845581_44572006_1_1_1_1,00.html#3 (accessed 27 September 2011).

Paelman, F. (2001) *CLIM: Coöperatief Leren in Multiculturele Groepen: CLIM-Wijzer* [Cooperative Learning in Multicultural Groups: CLIM Manual]. Ghent: Steunpunt Intercultureel Onderwijs – Universiteit Gent.

Parekh, B. (2006) *Rethinking Multiculturalism. Cultural diversity and political theory*, 2nd ed. Basingstoke: Palgrave Macmillan.

Ragnarsdóttir, H. (2008) *Collisions and Continuities: Ten immigrant families and their children in Icelandic society and schools*. Saarbrücken: VDM Verlag Dr. Müller.

— (2010) 'Internationally educated teachers and student teachers in Iceland: Two qualitative studies'. *Canadian Journal of Educational Administration and Policy*, 100. Online: www.umanitoba.ca/publications/cjeap/articles/Ragnarsdottir-iet. html (accessed 27 September 2011).

Ragnarsdóttir, H. and Blöndal, H. (2007) 'Háskólastigið í ljósi hnattvæðingar. Rannsókn á stöðu og reynslu erlendra nemenda við Kennaraháskóla Íslands'. *Uppeldi og menntun*, 16 (2), 161–82.

— (2010) 'Skólamenning og fjölbreyttir starfsmannahópar í leikskólum'. In Ragnarsdóttir, H. and Jónsdóttir, E.S. (eds) *Fjölmenning og skólastarf*. Reykjavík: Rannsóknastofa í fjölmenningarfræðum og Háskólaútgáfan.

Ragnarsdóttir, H. and Loftsdóttir, K. (2010) 'Námsefni og kennsluhættir í fjölmenningarlegu samfélagi'. In Ragnarsdóttir, H' and Jónsdóttir, E'S. (eds) *Fjölmenning og skólastarf*. Reykjavík: Rannsóknastofa í fjölmenningarfræðum og Háskólaútgáfan.

Reykjavíkurborg [City of Reykjavík] (2011a) *Stefna og starfsáætlun Menntasviðs Reykjavíkur*. Online. www.reykjavik.is/Portaldata/1/Resources/menntasvid/skjol/Starfsa_tlun_2011.pdf (accessed 27 October 2011).

— (2011b) *Reglur um samskipti leik- og grunnskóla og frístundaheimila Reykjavíkurborgar við trúar- og lífsskoðunarfélög*. Online. www.reykjavik.is/desktopdefault.aspx/tabid-3801/2281_read-28347/2281_page-2/ (accessed 26 October 2011).

— (2011c) *Nýir Íslendingar*. Online. reykjavik.is/desktopdefault.aspx/tabid-3806/6354_view-2327/ (accessed 7 November 2011).

Ryan, J. (2003) *Leading Diverse Schools*. Dordrecht: Kluwer.

Santoro, N. (2007) '"Outsiders" and "others": "Different" teachers teaching in culturally diverse classrooms'. *Teachers and Teaching: Theory and practice*, 13, 81–97.

Schmidt, C. and Block, L.A. (2010) 'Without and within: The implications of employment and ethnocultural equity policies for internationally educated teachers'. *Canadian Journal of Educational Administration and Policy.* 100. Online. www.umanitoba.ca/publications/cjeap/articles/schmidt-block-iet.html (accessed 27 September 2011).

Szkoła Polska w Reykjaviku [Polish School in Reykjavik] (2010) Personnel. Online. www.polskaszkola.is/ (accessed 27 October 2011).

UNESCO (2010) 'Education'. Online. www.unesco.org/en/esd/ (accessed 27 October 2011).

Vertovec, S. (2009) *Transnationalism.* London: Routledge.

Zielińska, M., Kowzan, P., and Ragnarsdóttir, H. (In press) 'Polish complementary schools in Iceland and England'. *Intercultural Education.*

Chapter 6

Individualistic strategies of teaching in relation to linguistic minority pupils' needs: A discussion based on fieldwork at Meadows School, Oslo, Norway

Thor Ola Engen

In Norway, the relatively low academic achievement scores of linguistic minority schoolchildren (pupils in primary and lower secondary school with a mother tongue other than Norwegian or Sami) compared to their Norwegian-speaking peers (Roe *et al.*, 2003; Bakken, 2007; Aasen *et al.*, 2003; Rydland, 2007) has caused concern as the proportion of minorities in the pupil population steadily increases.

In Oslo, where the proportion of linguistic minority schoolchildren now exceeds 35 per cent of all pupils in the city (Oslo kommune, Utdanningsetaten, hjemmeside [The Community of Oslo, School Administration, Home Page] 2006), the community school administration has encouraged new teaching strategies to better meet pupils' needs, and has initiated research projects to identify and promote cases of best practice.

One of these projects focused on four schools that had distinguished themselves by attaining the best national test scores of schools where 40–60 per cent of pupils belonged to a linguistic minority. Together with three colleagues, I spent two separate one-week periods at one of these schools, Meadows School, in an eastern suburb of Oslo in 2006–07. We conducted fieldwork at three grade levels: the initial stage, the middle stage, and the lower secondary stage. Classroom observations were made for ten days in all, and focus interviews were conducted with two groups of pupils, one from the middle stage and one from the lower secondary stage. Two teams of teachers, one from the middle and one from the lower secondary stage, were interviewed individually and in groups. In addition, the principal and the assistant principal were interviewed extensively, while other management representatives, together with selected teachers, were interviewed informally on several occasions, as we spent time between sessions and during lunchtime in the staff room or teachers' workplaces (Engen *et al.*, 2008).

Overview

The chapter begins by examining the broader socio-political and academic context of the study. Meadows School's preferred strategies are then discussed, based on case study material from all four researchers, which is equivalent to eight weeks of fieldwork. As representatives of Meadows School admitted, they were deeply concerned about one particular group of linguistic minority pupils, even though the school was producing good overall test results. Discussion of the background for the school's concern then follows, and I conclude by suggesting that Meadows School would have achieved even better scores on nationally administered tests if it had taken full account of the cultural and linguistic background of a broader group of its minority pupils.

Theoretical perspectives

Contemporary societies are defined by their ability constantly to change, specialize, and identify new tasks in a competitive international market, and to include different lifestyles, knowledge, and norms that occur side by side. At the same time, dramatic developments in communication and information technologies have weakened the authority of science and the school's monopoly of knowledge. It has consequently been argued that the implementation of national goals needs to be left to the schools themselves, separated from tradition as well as from the prescriptive power of central authorities (Baker, 2011; Krejsler, 2007). Around the beginning of the new millennium, education authorities in Norway started to delegate responsibility to schools, giving school leaders a new and more central role (Haug and Bachmann, 2007; Møller *et al.*, 2005). And in response to diversity, freedom, delegation, deregulation, decentralization, and competition, the national curriculum of 2006 replaced the traditional specific guidelines on content and learning materials with general overall objectives for the subjects, opening an even larger space of freedom for schools and school leaders (Engelsen and Karseth, 2007; Haug and Bachmann, 2007).

Schools thus came to be regarded as individual and relatively independent learning organizations, and were expected to develop organizational plans that could integrate staff, pupils, and parents by interacting closely with internal cultures. As part of a pedagogical rhetoric that claimed that the individual must learn to navigate in a complex and unpredictable world, the pupil as an individual agent assumed a central focus. On the one hand, pupils were expected to structure and carry out their own learning obligations, through different types of self-technologies; on the other hand, schools were expected to facilitate different strategies of individualization (Banks, 2008; Klette, 2007; Krejsler, 2007). The individualistic perspective as the dominant discourse for successful schools (Haug and Bachmann, 2007; Langer, 2004; Senge, 2000; Turmo, 2009) created a new context in which schools – Meadows School included – were expected to develop and improve their learning environments and teaching strategies.

The individualistic perspective tends to take the majority culture and language for granted (Engen, 2009). However, in a comprehensive longitudinal research project, Thomas and Collier (2002) demonstrated that the only educational programmes that allow linguistic minority pupils to close the achievement gap are the one-way and two-way bilingual models. Although mainstream programmes see linguistic minority pupils make substantial progress in their first three to four years of schooling, by the time they advance to the lower secondary stage, they are lagging behind the performance of their linguistic majority counterparts. In Norway, the national test scores of linguistic minority pupils are weaker in the seventh than in the second grade (Bonesrønning and Vaag Iversen, 2008). Thus, according to Thomas and Collier (*ibid.*) and Collier and Thomas (2009), mainstream programmes possess little potential as far as linguistic minority pupils' long-term academic performance is concerned, at least when they are unilaterally implemented.

The Threshold Hypothesis developed by Cummins (2000) explains the respective superiority and inferiority of bilingual models and mainstream programmes. While the first enable linguistic minority pupils to master both their native and second languages at a level appropriate for their age, the second leave many to function below it. As August and Hakuta (1997) have reported more generally, when education is adaptive to linguistic minority pupils' needs, schools provide identity confirmation by valuing those children's cultural and linguistic backgrounds and allow them to use their native language as an academic tool (cf. Christensen and Stanat, 2007; Taguma *et al.*, 2009). This argument may be nuanced further by Linell's statement: 'Sense-making always goes beyond the text or discourse itself and relates it to a background, a context' (Linell, 1992). Donaldson (1978) and Rommetveit (1974) have demonstrated, meanwhile, that children perform at their best both cognitively and linguistically in situations that have subjective meaning in their lives. According to Baker (2006), this is to be expected because it is always the experience, as well as the values and beliefs that we bring with us, that enable us to create meaning in what we are reading.

However, mainstream programmes sometimes yield better academic results than bilingual programmes. Simply valuing linguistic minority pupils' cultural and linguistic backgrounds is insufficient unless programmes are well implemented (Baker, 2011). In the research summarized by August and Hakuta (1997), school leaders focused specifically on the challenges that arise from linguistic minority pupils' learning contexts. For example, school leaders ensured that bilingual teachers and second-language teachers coordinated their efforts, and that all teachers – not only language teachers – were specially trained to teach linguistic minority pupils.

Meadows School placed an equally strong focus on the challenges that arose from linguistic minority pupils' learning situations. Their monolingual programme enabled such pupils to function at age level in one of their languages within a mainstream context. Since this is neither an advantage nor a disadvantage for learning, according to the Threshold Hypothesis, the programme could be deemed a success. The cultural and linguistic backgrounds of linguistic minority pupils were not valued at Meadows School, however, as these pupils were explicitly denied the opportunity to use their native language as an academic tool. For example, when a boy of Somali origin used his native language to try to collaborate with another boy of the same linguistic background during a work-plan session, he was interrupted by a rejecting and rather severe 'hush' from the teacher. The teacher's underlying attitude may have put up an unnecessary learning barrier – as highlighted at the end of this chapter.

The background for academic success: the perspectives of the school

Here I present the staff and management's perceptions of the measures that were most significant in raising Meadows School's national test scores. Virtually every one of the school's representatives singled out three factors: the use of the work-plans approach; the arrangement – and combination – of extracurricular study hours and specially designed courses for linguistic minority pupils; and a well-developed and well-managed school 'mediatheque' – i.e. a school library that contained printed and audio books, CDs, and DVDs for loan. I analyse these factors in relation to other interview and observation data and suggest that the measures emphasized by the school may also be considered as coordinated constituents of a systemic approach deeply rooted in its culture.

The work-plans approach

> I think the model that we have adopted in recent years has been beneficial not only with regard to differentiated work plans and education, but also in terms of offering something more than a full day's learning: that is, extra study time after regular school hours for those kids who do not receive the support that they need at home. I also think that the mediateque, which is well staffed and open every day, has had a positive impact.
>
> (Meadows School Assistant Principal)

According to our informants, in the course of a decade Meadows School had gradually gone from being a traditional school characterized by regular classroom instruction to a modern school that focuses mainly on individual pupil work. The approach chosen was based on so-called work plans, a methodological approach presented in greater detail below. It involved documents of instructions and assignments for all pupils at a certain grade level, collectively designed by a group of teachers (cf. Klette, 2007; Olaussen, 2009). At Meadows School the approach included the following subjects: Norwegian language; English; social studies; Christianity, religion, and beliefs; and science. Mathematics was no longer an integrated part of the curriculum as, according to the teachers' observations, too many pupils had elected to downgrade the subject.

Teachers were still expected to give lectures, but only as introductions to new themes at the beginning of work plan periods. The lectures were given for all pupils at one grade level, usually as many as 50–60. After the introductory lectures, pupils mainly worked individually with specially designed work-plan assignments for a period of two to three weeks. In these periods, the approach allowed pupils to choose *what* subject they wanted to work on, *how long* they wanted to spend working on it, and *when* the work should be done. It was a mandatory requirement, however, that all assignments be completed by the end of the work-plan period. Although the emphasis was on independent work, pupils were supervised. While some received individual assistance or guidance, according to articulated or sometimes non-articulated needs, the majority seemed to manage entirely on their own. Pupils with special needs were included in the work-plan approach, as the school management believed that the team of teachers collectively responsible for each grade level was suitably qualified to decide which pupils needed help and of what kind, and how available resources should be allocated.

Instruction was differentiated according to three criteria. As well as determining how much work they would do and at what pace, pupils could also choose between assignments with three different levels of complexity. Based on their test results and teachers' formal and informal assessments, pupils were advised about what level might suit them but it was up to each of them individually to make the final decision. The level chosen was not permanent, however, and pupils did not necessarily have to work at the same level for each subject. It was decided that all work-plan assignments should be distributed, submitted, and assessed via a digital online meeting place, which functioned as a school internal bulletin board and mailbox for teachers and pupils.

Extracurricular study hours, specially designed subject courses, and mediatheque

Immediately after the school day, Meadows School arranged for teachers to be available to offer guidance and support for an extra 75 minutes daily. Taking up this opportunity of additional time was voluntary, but 40 per cent of pupils did so – with linguistic minority pupils accounting for the greater number, although not all of them attended regularly.

During this extracurricular study period, Meadows School had also organized courses on specific subjects. These were primarily for pupils who struggled to meet the minimum requirements of the work-plan assignments.

> It also means that at times we offer courses to individual pupils in Norwegian, maths, and English ... Then there was the wish of the teachers [to] use the regular Norwegian schoolbooks, social science books, and science books, and it was more rewarding and the pupils felt it more meaningful.
>
> (Assistant Principal)

These courses were initially optional, but became mandatory when pupils committed to them. To begin with, they focused mainly on fundamental Norwegian language skills, but eventually looked at academic language and the vocabulary related to Norwegian language, English, and mathematics. The school's mediatheque, which offered varied materials, was also used extensively by linguistic minority pupils, and therefore offered an important supplement to what their homes had to offer, as reported by staff.

The mediatheque has seen a substantial increase in the lending of books ... The mediatheque... is also more frequently used by foreign language pupils than others.

(Ove, middle stage teacher)

The background for academic success: a researcher's perspective

To a certain extent, our informants were right to assume that the measures implemented at Meadows School contributed to improved test results. I argue, however, that such measures should be considered more as coordinated and integrated constituents of a systemic and culturally rooted approach than as isolated or independent features. I suggest that it was due to the management's consistent and systematic innovation that an organizational infrastructure for instruction, rooted in a local culture of teaching and learning, emerged at the school.

The organizational infrastructure for learning

And then we tried to create packages around the Meadows [School] model ... that all teachers would work on a certain stage, all teachers should have extended pupil responsibility, and they were sort of decentralized resources with a greater degree of autonomy, and so we should as management try to follow them up closer than before.

(Principal)

The organizational infrastructure for learning consisted of the following four elements:

- A team of cooperating teachers at each grade level – these teams had been given a major responsibility for planning, organizing, conducting, and assessing instruction.
- Extended working hours for teachers that corresponded to the pupils' extracurricular study period – this gave teachers extra time to supervise, assist, and guide the participating pupils' work systematically.
- A directly binding cooperation with the home, involving formal contracts with parents on pupils' participation in the extracurricular study period, and an increase in the number of parent–school meetings, which focused more clearly on the pupils' academic development. In this way, the school had managed to involve parents in the pupils'

academic work to a far greater extent than the formal home–school partnership allowed.

- An ICT-based instruction strategy, which was central to the work-plans approach and the school's self-perception and cultural image.

While these elements had been designed separately to support education as an individual enterprise within the work-plans approach, together they constituted an organizational infrastructure that may have contributed to Meadows School's academic results. Beyond giving teachers extra time for supervising individual pupils, the infrastructure allowed them to plan and collaborate with each other, distribute and manage resources more efficiently, and deepen professional communication. Staff reported that it also increased staff's commitment to fostering cooperation between the pupils' homes and the school:

> We talk a lot together. There are many informal conversations and exchanges in the staffroom, and it is probably very important. … because if it had not been for the experiment with extended working hours – so that we are all present at the same time – I think that cooperation would have been reduced a lot.
>
> I think the strength of our school [is] that we think differently, to be a little – shall we say – open to trying new things … to a much greater extent than many other schools. I have that feeling, anyway … I would say it seems so on the basis of the results we have had, for we have had a tremendous development in our school and have been creative compared to many others.
>
> (Isabel, lower secondary school teacher)

A local culture of teaching and learning

We might see the development of a shared way of thinking about education, both within each grade team and among the entire staff, as reflecting a local culture of learning and instruction – one that partly interacts with and partly reinforces the features of the organizational infrastructure. This culture was apparent in high learning expectations, which, according to both teachers and pupils, were contained 'in the walls' of the school. These learning expectations were also articulated explicitly, with the school's management closely following up on teachers' success when they helped pupils reach their goals. Management and teachers placed strong emphasis on results when speaking to the pupils and parents. In interviews, pupils demonstrated their awareness that achievement, especially in mathematics, English, and

Norwegian, was important – echoing the measured progress provided by the Oslo school administration as well as Meadows School. When five pupils in Grade 7 and three in Grade 8 were asked what they thought was most important to learn in school, they said:

> *Pupil 1 (Grade 7)*: Everything, really.
> *Interviewer*: If you had asked your mom and dad, what do you think they would have said?
> *Pupil 2*: Norwegian and maths and English!
> Interviewer: Do you agree?
> *The five Grade 7 pupils*: Yes!
> *Pupil 3* (Grade 8): Everything that we learn, really, I think is important. It is something that is more important than other things, though.
> *Interviewer*: What is that, then?
> *Pupil 4 (Grade 8)*: It is three subjects: maths, English, and Norwegian!

The local culture of learning and instruction was reinforced by the emphasis on teachers' academic qualifications, which had been incorporated into the school's policy of recruitment.

> So, here [at Meadows School] we have in recent years put more emphasis on bringing in people with the right academic background. I think management has been clever when it comes to hand-pick[ing] people who have the right professional expertise, [the kind that they] are missing, or which is scarce. I think, they've been very conscious of that.
>
> (Ove, middle stage teacher)

While applicants' individual academic competences were taken into consideration, how well they would complement their potential grade team colleagues was also given due thought. Neither the emphasis on teachers' academic qualifications nor the articulated learning expectations are obvious priorities in Norwegian primary schools (Klette, 2003).

Systematic innovation

When Norwegian government education ministers delegated responsibility and influence to individual institutions around the start of the new millennium, the principal at Meadows School seized the opportunity vigorously and effectively, according to our teacher informants. He first established a vision and potential identity for the school that would unify both staff and pupils:

The starting point was: how should we profile ourselves? We should develop our pedagogy and then we should all have one or two guiding stars ... we should be a unified school instead of being such a fragmented school. That was number one. ... [We should] find some main focus point, and we had many [teachers] who were interested in ICT .... Visiting other schools, we also noticed that ICT was a powerful agent with regard to differentiation at pupil level, and when applied to monitoring. Thus, it had several purposes, and was probably bigger than we thought at the time. But now it's almost like ICT has become the solution and that makes me very nervous ... .

(Principal)

After some discussion, a vision for The ICT School was determined; influential teachers put forward the idea not just out of personal interest and skill but also because they believed that ICT could facilitate pedagogical differentiation and present the school as a modern, future-oriented institution. Over time it also appeared that access to computers might enhance pupils' academic motivation and achievement in Norwegian (cf. Grøgaard *et al.*, 2008).

However, our informants did not believe that the school's culture had developed primarily as a result of any visionary decision. Both the staff and management felt that the school's organizational infrastructure was gradually built up. Our informants unanimously recognized that a local culture of learning and instruction had followed a shift away from entrenched practices and simplistic attitudes. Many new initiatives had been so controversial that some teachers had chosen to leave the school. However, as more teachers took part in the programmme of innovation, a resistant atmosphere in the school was gradually replaced by constructive and forward thinking – and the staff were now ready to use their creativity to offer alternative solutions.

Discussion

So-called self-technologies position the autonomous, self-realizing, and self-regulating learner at both the starting point and the goal of the learning process. They are tailor-made for highly motivated children, such as those from families of middle-class professionals (Bourdieu and Passeron, 1990; Krejsler, 2007) – who are, indeed, the most successful pupils in Norwegian schools (Bonesrønning and Vaag Iversen, 2008). According to Meadows School informants, the work-plans approach was no exception; it favours conscientious and self-disciplined middle-class pupils – including those from linguistic minorities – who have a culture of learning at home (Engen,

2009). Lidén (2001) has shown that teaching styles can expand pupils' proximal development zone as greatly as they can reduce it (cf. Heath, 1986; Vygotsky, 1987).

Teachers and management representatives were in agreement that if the work-plans approach was implemented unilaterally, it would not erase differences between pupils but would instead be more likely to reinforce the difficulties faced by the academically weakest and least motivated of the linguistic majority pupils (Klette, 2007; Krejsler, 2007). In addition, the approach was not designed to meet the needs of pupils from culturally and linguistically diverse backgrounds:

> Weak pupils, in the old days – they hid away. But I see now that many of them are very willing to work and would like to have more help ... Nevertheless ... [the work-plans] approach probably works best for the academically strong and motivated school pupils ... [It is] probably better for talented and conscientious pupils, so we should find a way to cater for the more disorderly ones.
>
> (Ove, middle stage teacher)

Such differences between pupils led Meadows School to supplement the work-plans approach with extracurricular study periods. These were primarily for the large number of linguistic minority pupils who needed additional time and closer guidance to fulfil the requirements of the work plans. As the extracurricular study periods were voluntary, however, they also required the pupils to have high self-motivation. It was therefore assumed that the linguistic minority pupils who attended the extra study periods were those who felt that they could complete the work-plan assignments provided that they received the qualified help at school that most could not get at home. If we take this factor into account, it seems reasonable to infer that the extracurricular study periods provided an independent contribution in raising the school's average test scores (cf. Grøgaard *et al.*, 2008). Unfortunately, there is no quantitative data to corroborate this assumption, as Norwegian authorities do not publish test scores that take account of pupils' ethnic or linguistic backgrounds.

For pupils who felt that the work-plan assignments were out of their reach, Meadows School designed particular courses that specifically aimed to strengthen fundamental literacy skills. School representatives assumed that this measure brought the least demanding work-plan level into the proximal development zone of some of these pupils, an assumption supported by Øzerk (2009).

The data suggest that, by means of the work-plans approach, extracurricular study hours, and specifically designed courses in particular subjects, Meadows School managed to improve pupils' performance in national tests. Since the measures were embedded in a strong organizational infrastructure and culture for learning, it is likely that they also benefited pupils without academic support at home (Grøgaard *et al.*, 2008; cf. Bakken, 2009), indicating that the school's monolingual programme was well implemented.

The sociocultural perspective at Meadows School

Even when it is well implemented, an individualized programme such as that used at Meadows School tends to take for granted the majority culture and language. This may explain why the academic performance of the linguistic minority pupils was significantly lower than that of their Norwegian-speaking peers. It follows that even acceptable average achievement scores may not constitute a reliable indicator of the quality of instruction (Nordahl, 2009). When inter-school achievement differences contrast mainly with intra-school variations – when the former are relatively small and the latter quite substantial – average scores may obscure quite noticeable intra-school variations (Bakken, 2009; Grøgaard *et al.*, 2008).

This may have been the case at Meadows School. According to our informants, it was only the pupils who participated in the specially designed courses and a few who were helped by the extracurricular study hours who went on to perform at the most demanding work-plan level. In the interviews, these staff observers expressed special concern about those linguistic minority pupils who had arrived when of school age and whose parents, according to the school, had weak educational backgrounds or poor Norwegian language proficiency. Staff representatives from Meadows School admitted that these pupils found it hard to benefit from its strategies; what they actually needed was bilingual education. However, rather than encouraging bilingual teaching and engaging bilingual teachers, the school not only ignored sociocultural differences but also tried to obliterate them by invoking the community school administration mantra that 'a pupil is a pupil'. That key differences between pupils had been overlooked became apparent when teachers had to consult admission documents before they could tell the researchers how many native languages were spoken at the school. Pupil informants, by contrast, answered the question without much hesitation.

The reason why pupils who, according to the school's own analysis, needed bilingual education were not given that opportunity may of course be interpreted in many ways and on different theoretical levels (Engen, 2010a).

Here, I focus on the school's strategic reasoning, related to the performance indicators of the community school administration, which were recognized by the teachers and pupils.

When compared to the other schools in Oslo, Meadows School's performance level was somewhat below average. This suggests that a greater number of pupils were struggling at Meadows. The school itself, however, did not think in such terms, taking schools with a similar demographic profile as their obvious point of reference. The same bases for comparison were used by the school authorities as criteria for initiating the research project. Apparently, neither the school management, the teachers, nor the community authorities really believed that scores closer to those of the highest-performing schools were realistic at schools with a relatively large proportion of minority pupils. Compared to schools with a similar demographic profile, however, Meadows School had reduced both the grade gap between linguistic majority and minority pupils and the proportion of seriously low achievers. By doing so, it had increased the proportion of linguistic minority pupils responding to mainstream instruction, which is why it was selected as a case study. Even though at Meadows School the proportion of pupils that were struggling was higher than at other schools, it is likely that pupils at the latter were functioning on a higher level than those at schools with a similar demographic profile. By limiting the frame of reference to schools with a similar demographic profile, Meadows' management and teachers saw no need for bilingual teaching for a marginal group of linguistic minority pupils.

This line of strategic reasoning is highly problematic, however. According to Section 2–8 of Norway's Education Act (1998), pupils with a first language other than Norwegian who lack sufficient Norwegian language skills to profit from mainstream instruction have not only a right to specially adapted instruction in the Norwegian language but, if necessary, are also entitled to home language instruction or bilingual subject instruction, or both, for as long as it takes them to develop the proficiency required to join the mainstream. A key consideration, then, is for pupils to have sufficient language skills to join the mainstream (Øzerk, 2007).

A comprehensive response to the law suggests that pupils are given equal opportunities, according to professional judgement, to realize their learning and development potential, thus enabling them to function academically and linguistically according to their age level (Engen, 2010b). This was certainly not the case for the designated group at Meadows School, and probably not for a wider group of linguistic minority pupils either, as implied above.

Such provision was notably denied to the aforementioned group of pupils at Meadows School, and most likely affected a wider group of linguistic minority pupils as well. Within the school's culture of alternative solutions, the sociocultural perspective was only implicit and took only the strongly self-motivated middle-class pupils into account. Because subject content was mistakenly seen as being culture-free and accessible to all, these pupils were continuously favoured by the work-plans approach.

To enable linguistic minority pupils to function at a level closer to their age, Meadows School needs to expand its sociocultural perspective on education and make it more explicit. An interview with a linguistic minority boy in Grade 7, whom teachers deemed representative of the group who struggled academically, supports these recommendations.

When asked about his reading habits, the boy stated that he had read only one book in his whole life. But the book was not an easy reader, as might be expected, but was about the US boxer, Cassius Clay, who converted to Islam and changed his name to Muhammad Ali after winning the world heavyweight championship in 1964. His voluntary reading was restricted to 'soccer magazines'. When asked about his favourite players, the boy mentioned Ramiro Corrales, a Mexican–American who plays for a local Norwegian team.

We thought that Corrales and particularly Ali, the idolized and vilified cultural icon, seemed highly attractive identity models for a second-generation immigrant boy of colour. On the one hand, the boy mentioned Corrales, who, although a competent footballer, seldom appeared in the media. On the other hand, when we suggested that the book about Ali probably contained a lot of words that he might find difficult in light of his academic performance, he maintained that he 'liked to read it'. In any case, both Ali and Corrales certainly appeared more attractive to this boy than Per, Paul, and Espen, characters who appear in many of the Norwegian fairy tales that were the main topic of school assignments during one of the weeks that we spent at Meadows School. The interview sends a message about the importance of the sociocultural perspective. As sense-making always goes beyond the text or discourse itself, to enable them to relate what they are reading to a credible context, linguistic minority pupils should be given subject matter that provides greater identity verification than we saw at Meadows School. Greater relevance can engage pupils' intrinsic motivation (Cummins, 2004), contribute to changing their attitudes towards reading in general (cf. Schecter and Cummins, 2003; Taguma *et al.*, 2009), and thus strengthen their reading skills as well as expanding their vocabulary and sociocultural knowledge.

Recommendations

In addition to expanding the range of criteria for selecting academic content, there are several other ways that Meadows School's mainly individualized approach could be improved by taking a sociocultural perspective on education. Three examples are offered here. First, as the school itself recognizes, the linguistic minority pupils who had the greatest problems with the strategies that the school adopted would probably have developed fundamental reading skills more easily if their first language had been utilized in their fundamental reading instruction (Baker, 2006; Schecter and Cummins, 2003). But it is also probable that far more linguistic minority pupils would have profited from such an approach, so reducing the need for the kind of special courses provided.

Secondly, instead of rejecting the Somali boy's suggestion that he collaborate with another boy of the same linguistic background, the teacher might have done better to support his initiative. As Schecter and Cummins (2003) have demonstrated, linguistic minority pupils who are encouraged to use their first language as a working tool and in pupil–pupil collaboration are enabled to function more closely to their age level both cognitively and linguistically. This has proved to be the case even when they are required to report their final results in the majority language.

Thirdly, teacher–pupil conversations about majority-language textbook material indicate that pupils' first language may be a powerful instrument (Engen, 2009; Ryen *et al.*, 2005). Even if such an approach requires bilingual teachers, it would nevertheless have been valuable in the extracurricular study periods related to work-plan assignments at Meadows School, and even more helpful in the specially designed subject courses with their emphasis on academic language and vocabulary. In all three cases, pupils would probably have been enabled to function both academically and linguistically more closely to their age level, thus contributing far more to raising the school's average scores.

Conclusion

Through consistent innovation, Meadows School has established an organizational infrastructure and a local culture for teaching and learning, both of which have helped the school in its efforts to raise its pupils' mean scores on national tests, compared to schools with a similar demographic profile. However, the dominant individualistic perspective, with its implicit bias towards the cultural majority, may have led the school to neglect the educational needs of linguistic minority pupils in general, and especially those with a non-academic home background or those having only recently arrived in the host country. If a selective but also systematic use of the home language had been an integrated part of the organizational infrastructure for learning, as exemplified above, we believe that, in national tests, Meadows School could have come closer to the average scores of all Oslo's schools, and not merely been one of the best among schools with a comparable demographic.

References

Aasen, J., Engen, T.O., and Nes, K. (2003) '*Ved nåløyet: rapport fra konferansen "Hvordan klarer minoritetselevene seg i skolen?"*': Hamar 16–18 September 2002, Rapport/ Høgskolen i Hedmark. Elverum: Høgskolen i Hedmark.

August, D. and Hakuta, K. (eds) (1997) *Improving Schooling for Language Minority Children: A research agenda*. Washington, DC: National Academy Press.

Baker, C. (2006) *Foundations of Bilingual Education and Bilingualism: Bilingual education and bilingualism*, 4th ed. Clevedon: Multilingual Matters.

— (2011) *Foundations of Bilingual Education and Bilingualism*. Bristol: Multilingual Matters.

Bakken, A. (2007) *Virkninger av Tilpasset Språkopplæring for Minoritetsspråklige Elever: En kunnskapsoversikt*. Oslo: Norsk institutt for forskning om oppvekst, velferd og aldring (NOVA).

— (2009) *Ulikhet På Tvers: Har foreldres utdanning, kjønn og minoritetsstatus like stor betydning for elevers karakterer på alle skoler? NOVA rapport*. Oslo: NOVA.

Banks, J.A. (2008) 'Diversity, group identity, and citizenship education in a global age'. *Educational Researcher*, 37 (3), 129–39.

Bonesrønning, H. and Vaag Iversen, J.M. (2008) *Suksessfaktorer i Grunnskolen: analyse av nasjonale prøver 2007* no. 05/08. Trondheim: Senter for økonomisk forskning AS.

Bourdieu, P. and Passeron, J.C. (1990) *Reproduction in Education, Society and Culture*, 2nd ed. London: Sage.

Christensen, G. and Stanat, P. (2007) *Language Policies and Practices for Helping Immigrants and Second Generation Students Succeed*. Migration Policy Institute, Bertelsmann.

Collier, V.P. and Thomas, W.P. (2009) *Educating English Learners for a Transformed World*. Albuquerque: Fuente Press.

Cummins, J. (2000) *Language, Power and Pedagogy: Bilingual children in the crossfire* (Bilingual education and bilingualism 23). Clevedon: Multilingual Matters.

— (2004) 'Multiliteracies pedagogy and the role of identity texts'. In Leithwood, K., McAdie, P., Bascia, N., and Rodigue, A. (eds) *Teaching for Deep Understanding: Towards the Ontario curriculum that we need*. Toronto: Ontario Institute for Studies in Education of the University of Toronto and the Elementary Federation of Teachers of Ontario.

Donaldson, M. (1978) *Children's Minds*. Glasgow: Fontana/Collins.

Engelsen, B.U. and Karseth, B. (2007) 'Læreplan for kunnskapsløftet - endret kunnskapssyn'. *Norsk Pedagogisk Tidskrift*, 91 (5), 404–15.

Engen, T.O. (2009) 'Three major strategies of adaptive instruction for LMi-students'. In Ringen, B.-K., Kjørven, O.K., and Gagné, A. (eds) *Teacher Diversity in a Diverse School: Challenges and opportunities for teacher education*. Vallset: Oplandske Bokforlag.

— (2010a) 'Literacy instruction and integration: The case of Norway'. *Intercultural Education (European Journal of Intercultural Studies)*, 1, 171–83.

— (2010b) 'Viss den brede vei blir den smale sti. Om lovgrunnlaget for tilpasset opplæring for minoritetsspråklige elever'. In Johansen, H., Golden, A., Hagen, J.E., and Helland, A.-K. (eds) *Systematisk, Variert, men ikke Tilfeldig: Antologi om norsk som andrespråk I anledning Kari Tenfjords 60-årsdag*. Oslo: Novus.

Engen, T.O., Kulbrandstad, L.A., Kulbrandstad, L.I., Danbolt, A.M.V., and Bakke, E. (2008) *Oppsummerende Rapport*. Hamar: Høgskolen i Hedmark.

Grøgaard, J.B., Helland, H., and Lauglo, J. (2008) *Elevenes læringsutbytte: hvor stor betydning har skolen? En analyse av ulikhet i elevers prestasjonsnivå i fjerde, syvende og tiende trinn i grunnskolen og i grunnkurset i videregående*. Oslo: NIFU STEP Norsk institutt for studier av innovasjon, forskning og utdanning.

Haug, P. and Bachmann, K.E. (2007) 'Kvalitet og tilpasning'. *Norsk Pedagogisk Tidskrift*, 91 (4), 265–76.

Heath, S.H. (1986) 'Sociocultural contexts of language development'. In Bilingual Education Office (ed.) *Beyond Language: Social and cultural factors in schooling language minority students*. Los Angeles: California State University.

Klette, K. (2003) *Klasserommets Praksisformer etter Reform 97*. Oslo: Pedagogisk forskningsinstitutt.

— (2007) 'Bruk av arbeidsplaner i skolen – et hovedverktøy for å realisere tilpasset opplæring?' *Norsk Pedagogisk Tidsskrift*, 91(4), 344–58.

Krejsler, J. (2007) 'Skolereform, livslang læring og individualisering'. *Norsk Pedagogisk Tidsskrift*, 91 (4), 277–89.

Langer, J.A. (2004) *Getting to Excellent: How to create better schools*. New York: Teachers College Press.

Lidén, H. (2001) 'Underforstått likhet. Skolens håndtering av forskjeller i et flerkulturelt samfunn'. In Lien, M.E., Lidén, H., and Vike, H. (eds) *Likhetens Paradokser: Antropologiske undersøkelser i det moderne Norge*. Oslo: Universitetsforlaget.

Linell, P. (1992) 'The embeddedness of decontextualisation in the context of social practices'. In Wold, A.H. (ed.) *The Dialogical Alternative: Towards a theory of language and mind*. Oslo: Scandinavian University Press.

Møller, J., Eggen, A., Fuglestad, O.L., Langfeldt, G., Presthus, A., Skrøvset, A., Stjernstrøm, S., and Vedøy, G. (2005) 'Successful school leadership: The Norwegian case'. *Journal of Educational Administration*, 43 (6), 584–94.

Nordahl, T. (2009) 'Barnets rett til utdanning og realiteter i norsk skole'. In Hjerman, R. and Haanes, K. (eds) *Barn*. Oslo: Universitetsforlaget.

Olaussen, S.B. (2009) 'Arbeidsplaner i skolen: En kontekst for utvikling av selvregulert læring? Refleksjoner etter en studie på småskoletrinnet'. *Norsk Pedagogisk Tidsskrift*, 93 (3), 189–201.

Oslo kommune, Utdanningsetaten, hjemmeside [Community of Oslo, School Administration, Home Page] (2006). Online. http://tinyurl.com/kumu3ta

Øzerk, K.Z. (2007) *Avvik og Merknad*. Vallset: Oplandske Bokforlag.

— (2009) 'Læring av lærestoff og utvikling av språk på skolen'. *Norsk Pedagogisk Tidsskrif*, (4), 294–309.

Roe, A., Linnakylä, P., and Lie, S. (2003) *Northern Lights on PISA: Unity and diversity in the Nordic countries in PISA 2000*. Oslo: Department of Teacher Education and School Development, University of Oslo.

Rommetveit, R. (1974) *On Message Structure: A framework for the study of language and communication*. London: Wiley.

Rydland, V. (2007) 'Minoritetsspråklige elevers skoleprestasjoner: hva sier empirisk forskning?' *Acta Didactica Norge* 1 (1). Online. http://adno.no/index.php/adno/article/viewArticle/16/52 (accessed 1 April 2012).

Ryen, E., Wold, A.H., and de Wal Pastoor, L. (2005) 'Det er egen tolkning, ikke direkte regler. Kasusstudier av minoritesspråklige elevers morsmålsopplæring og bruk av morsmål ved tre grunnskoler'. *NOA norsk som andrespråk*, 21 (1–2) 39–66.

Schecter, S.R. and Cummins, J. (eds) (2003) *Multilingual Education in Practice: Using diversity as a resource*. Portsmouth, NH: Heinemann.

Senge, P.M. (2000) *Schools That Learn: Fifth discipline resource*. London: Nicholas Brealey.

Taguma, M., Shewbridge, C., Huttova, J., and Hoffman, N. (2009) *OECD Reviews of Migrant Education*. Norway, OECD.

Thomas, W.P. and Collier, V.P. (2002) *A National Study of School Effectiveness for Linguistic Minority Students' Long-term Academic Achievement*. Santa Cruz: CREDE.

Turmo, A. (2009) 'Internasjonale elevundersøkelser: Trender og fortolkninger'. In Raabe, M., Turmo, A., Vibe, N., Kirkebøen, L.J., and Steffensen, K. (eds) *Utdanning 2009: læringsutbytte og kompetanse*. Oslo/Kongsvnger: Statistisk Sentralbyrå.

Vygotsky, L.S. (1987) 'Thinking and speech'. In Rieber, R.W. and Carton, A.S. (eds) *The Collected Works of L.S. Vygotsky*. New York: Plenum Press.

Chapter 7

Becoming multilingual: Bridges and barriers to change in a monolingual primary and secondary school in Scotland

Geri Smyth and Nathalie Sheridan

The purpose of the two research projects discussed in this chapter was to investigate how schools, teachers, and pupils work together in a changing demographic context to ensure that education in Scotland really does provide equal opportunities for all pupils, regardless of the linguistic, educational, and socioeconomic realities of their backgrounds.

National context

In this chapter we discuss the ways in which one primary and one secondary school in Scotland responded to demographic change, and we draw out implications for developing good practice that will give all pupils and teachers agency within the school institution. Since 1999, Scotland has had a devolved parliament, with control over, among other areas, education. However, control of migration and asylum policy still rests with the UK Parliament. The Scottish government has attempted to adopt a stance towards immigration that is different from, and more welcoming than, the restrictive policy that UK legislation allows. It has adopted the slogan *One Scotland Many Cultures* to represent its orientation towards the cultural, ethnic, and linguistic diversity within the country (Scottish Government, 2007).

Schooling in Scotland is compulsory for 5–16-year-olds and is organized in a two-tier system: seven years of primary school, for 5–11-year-olds, taught by class teachers; and up to six years of secondary school, for 12–18-year-olds, taught by subject teachers. A high proportion of schooling in Scotland is free of charge and under local authority control; only 4.31 per cent of pupils are educated in the independent education sector (Scottish

Government, 2011a). For the most part English is the language of education, although there are a small number of Gaelic-language schools.

Owing to demographic changes brought about by global political and economic factors, the current linguistic demography of Scottish schools includes more than 30,000 pupils for whom English is not their first language. Pupils in Scottish schools between them speak 138 different languages, the most common of these after English being Polish, Urdu, Punjabi, and Arabic (Scottish Government, 2011b). Less than 2 per cent of teachers in Scotland are from an ethnic minority background. An unquantified but very small number of teachers use more than one language in their daily lives and even fewer use more than one language in their professional lives (Smyth, 2010). Thus the reality of the demographic context in which schooling is provided in Scotland is at odds with the aspirations of the Scottish government. It suggests that *Many Schools One Culture* amounts to the anglophone white Christian culture of the hegemonic mainstream.

The research described in this chapter took place during a period of significant demographic change in Scotland. The UK Immigration and Asylum Act (1999) had resulted in asylum-seekers in the UK being widely dispersed to local authorities who had agreed to provide housing, education, and social care for these people in return for financial support from the UK government. In 2000 the National Asylum Support Service (NASS) was established to administer this new system, and the City of Glasgow was the only local authority in Scotland that agreed to receive asylum-seekers under this programme. This led to the creation of the Glasgow Asylum Seeker Support Project (GASSP), whose aim was to ensure that asylum-seekers in Glasgow had access to housing, education, health, and social services. Between 2000 and 2005 more than 10,000 asylum-seekers arrived in Glasgow, and the children of these families were enrolled in Glasgow schools.

By 2008 there were 2,208 asylum-seeking and refugee children attending schools in Glasgow. GASSP was funded directly via NASS, and schools that accepted asylum-seekers were given additional funding, also through NASS, to develop their educational provision for the children of asylum-seekers. This educational investment created what became known as bilingual units in 28 primary or secondary schools in the city. The units were staffed by additional teachers who were specifically employed to teach English as an additional language (EAL). They aimed to provide support for the children of asylum-seekers as they made the transition to attending school in Scotland. Setting these units within the schools indicated that the local authority's goal was to achieve educational integration and mainstreaming as quickly as possible (Smyth, 2006a and b).

We conducted ethnographic research in two schools – one primary and one secondary – with these bilingual units from 2003 to 2005 (a primary and a secondary school) and 2008 to 2009 (a secondary school). We describe these periods as Phase 1 and Phase 2 of the project. Our research aimed to investigate the children's creative ways of responding to their new language, culture, and education system and to investigate the school's response to demographic change.

School contexts

According to statistics concerning levels of health, education, employment, and housing, Glasgow is the city with the highest degree of deprivation in Scotland (Scottish Government, 2009). Research has demonstrated that asylum-seekers and refugees may be perceived as a threat by local residents in zones of high social and economic deprivation (Lewis, 2006; Wren, 2004), yet in the UK it is in these very areas that asylum-seekers are most likely to be found.

Lady Jane Grey Primary School was built at the beginning of the twentieth century in one of the most socially deprived areas of Glasgow. The families of children attending the school lived in social housing, in blocks of flats that were 20 storeys high and due for demolition around the time of our research. Families seeking asylum were housed in these flats alongside families suffering from multiple deprivation, including unemployment and high crime rates. Prior to their arrival, the school population – both pupils and teachers – was exclusively English-speaking, but the new arrivals brought 17 new languages to the school almost overnight. Three new specialist teachers were consequently employed by the bilingual unit in the school.

Stringchurch Secondary School is in an area of Glasgow that was developed in the 1950s to provide more social housing for people from the overcrowded inner city. Though it was initially intended to provide only social housing, many of the houses are now privately owned following the controversial Right to Buy policy. The area lies within the 15 per cent most socially deprived areas in Scotland (Scottish Government, 2009) and suffers from the impact of territorialism and gang culture (Scottish Government, 2008) – one reason for the community's limited mobility. Fear of straying into other territories has led many local children to remain within their immediate area and has left them with little knowledge of the basic geography of their city. In contrast, the newly arrived pupils from refugee families were involved in networks and organizations across the city and had a greater knowledge of its public transport systems.

In 2002, teaching began in Stringchurch Secondary School's new building, which was purpose-built after the old school was demolished during the area's redevelopment. In June 2008 the school had 90 bilingual pupils; by 2009 the number had dropped to 60. The number of EAL teachers also fell – from three to only one: Mr Gee. He said that the decrease was mostly due to families receiving leave to remain in the UK and moving from the school catchment area. Only ten asylum-seeking families remained at this time. Furthermore, the bilingual units that had previously been set up were due to close and the EAL teachers would be dispersed to schools throughout the city.

Theoretical background

Field and habitus

The complexities of the changes to demography and school focus required the authors to employ a complex range of theoretical tools. We found the work of Bourdieu (1997b) on capital, field, habitus, and agency particularly useful as we engaged with the data and developed our understandings of how the schools and the pupils were responding to change.[1] The habitus – or dispositions – of individuals is shaped by their past and present circumstances, but it also shapes their present and future experiences. In our study we considered the children as they negotiated the habitus of the school pupil. For new arrivals to be integrated swifty, their social and cultural capital needed to be recognized, valued, and developed, and the assets they brought with them to the new habitus and field identified in terms of their linguistic and cultural knowledge bases and existing networks.

Schools placed a particular emphasis on enabling pupils to develop their social networks. In many cases pupils had been denied education prior to arriving in Scotland, for reasons associated with their families' decision to flee their country of origin, in some cases because of civil war. The children had therefore never inhabited the habitus of the pupil, so that, as they started school in Scotland, they encountered not only a new system but a completely new set of understandings and behaviours. Such transitions and adjustments were played out in the field of the school – a field where the majority of inhabitants already knew the norms and values. The norms and values espoused by education in Scotland are fundamentally connected to issues of social justice and equity – and are thus conducive to the integration of new arrivals, at least superficially. However, in this chapter we take the stance that integration is a two-way process, not merely an assimiliation of the new into the old.

Norms and values are subject to change depending on the economic and political climate of the time. The current climate of education globally fosters performance-based activity to respond to the sector's increasing marketization (Ball, 2000; Jeffrey, 2002) and the demands for improved assessment results, measured on a global basis. This creates huge tensions for teachers in schools where many pupils are new not only to the language but to the very role of pupil and the concept of school. The amount of agency that individual actors – in this case teachers and pupils – can operate is dependent on external factors. Reay (1998) has argued that schools have an identifiable institutional habitus that is shaped and reshaped by external socioeconomic processes. The habitus of individual teachers and pupils may find itself in conflict with a changing institutional habitus.

Power relations in school

Cummins's (2000) conceptualization of collaborative and coercive relations of power in schools and classrooms helped us understand the educational realities that we encountered and characterize the schools and classrooms in ways that help us to subsequently describe good practice. This theoretical background provided us with a framework to examine teachers' and pupils' realities in a changing institutional habitus and determine the ways that capitals were utilized to produce collaborative relations of power. These theoretical connections are shown in Figure 7.1.

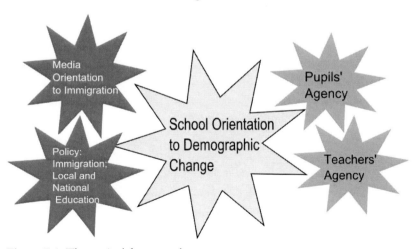

Figure 7.1: Theoretical framework

National policy on immigration and local and national policy on education affect the school's orientation towards demographic change. The school, as embodied by management, will promote relatively coercive or collaborative relationships of power, depending on the dominant discourse. This influences the amount of agency teachers have in their day-to-day interaction with pupils – who are affected in turn. The school's linguistic orientation towards immigrants will also affect the way schools respond to demographic change, and furthermore how migrant pupils perceive themselves within the school and the community.

Creative learning and teaching

To analyse the day-to-day learning and teaching that we observed during our fieldwork, we used Jeffrey and Woods's (2009) theoretical approach to creative learning and teaching, with its focus on learner agency, intersubjectivity, and participatory strategies. The strategies suggested in the concepts of creative learning and teaching are consistent with the aim of overcoming inequalities in power and abilities, as the focus is on the learners and their agency within the learning process and environment.

In the matter of creative learning and teaching, we do not interpret creativity as being associated with artistic disciplines (Claxton, 2006; Csikszentmihalyi, 1997; Gardner, 1993; Gauntlett, 2007; NACCCE, 1999) but rather as a *process that can be mobilized across much wider domains* (Csikszentmihalyi, 1997; Facer and Williamson, 2002: 4). Some of the most significant strategies for creativity are collaboration with others, intersubjectivity, intent, and purpose of activities, making use of knowledge in the domain of activity and the ability to draw on previous experiences (Csikszentmihalyi, 1997; Facer and Williamson, 2002; Jeffrey and Woods, 2009). Jeffrey (2006) has also found that social identity and belonging have a significant impact on positive learning identities, while Cummins (2001) emphasizes that only the assertion of pupil identities by teachers will ensure a successful negotiation of knowledge. Identity, language, and culture impact not only on learning in general but also on successful identity negotiation and inclusion (Bourdieu, 1977b; Bucholtz and Hall, 2004). Identity work is an ongoing process in which we perpetually negotiate and evaluate our different identities in relation and reaction to the social environment (Cummins, 2001; Hall, 1993; Keupp *et al.*, 2006). The concept of creative learning considers the physical, cognitive, and social processes that are involved in the learning process and that enabled us to consider the most advantageous practices for diverse pupils from a range of linguistic, cultural, and ethnic backgrounds.

Jeffrey and Woods (2009) established four prerequisites for creative learning and teaching: relevance, control, ownership, and innovation. In creative learning, pupils utilize and experience these characteristics, while teachers make use of these strategies to inform their pedagogy, providing a learning environment in which pupils can experience creative learning strategies and utilize them for their personal development. It was beneficial for us to make use of this theory to interrogate daily classroom practices all the while maintaining an awareness of the macro influences informing these classroom practices.

Relevance within a learning situation refers to the impact that the learning content has on the life of the pupil. It also encompasses positive social relations, described by Jeffrey and Woods (*ibid.*) as the trust that pupils have in their teachers and the commitment that teachers have to their pupils. Control refers to the impact the pupil has on the learning situation and, furthermore, to peer support and scaffolding by significant others. Ownership derives from the relevance and control of the learning process; the learning process becomes personalized by and makes sense to the pupil, and the relevance of the learning content becomes internalized and meaningful to him or her. The negotiation between the individual learning contents and the learning environment aims to create this ownership. Innovation does not necessarily refer to groundbreaking new findings, but rather to the process of change effected through learning and the pupils' ability to apply their newly acquired knowledge or skills. This is of particular significance when considering the learning of pupils new to the language of education and often to formalized school education itself. This approach to learning was highly appropriate for evaluating the pedagogy adopted by teachers in the new situations they found themselves in. It also merged well with our use of Bourdieu's and Cummins's work.

Methodology

Both phases of our research were conducted as ethnographic investigations. Ethnography understands the researcher as an instrument who uses multiple explorative methods to remain flexible to the demands of the field (Walford, 2008). We immersed ourselves in the field for a significant period of time, spreading our field visits across a whole school year or longer. The methods we applied were participant observation, field notes, semi-structured interviews, unstructured conversations with participants – teachers, pupils, school management, and other school staff – photographs taken by the pupil participants, group discussions, and researcher diaries. These methods allowed us to experience the day-to-day life of different learning spaces. Alongside the data collection, we analysed ongoing media debates and policy developments concerning education and immigration. This chapter presents only a small sample, drawn largely from researcher field notes and teacher interviews, of the full corpus we collected, as our purpose is to consider the changes that affected the school as its demography changed. Other work has utilized additional data for different purposes. See, for example, Smyth (2006a and b) and Smyth *et al.* (2010).

Phase 1 of the research took place primarily in Lady Jane Grey Primary School over 18 months, with field visits two to three times per week. The school's seven classes and bilingual unit were all sites of research, as were the staff room and outside school visits. Stringchurch Secondary School's staff room and bilingual unit were also part of this phase, as were the extracurricular activities involving pupils from the school. Phase 2 of the research took place in three learning spaces at Stringchurch Secondary School: the EAL (bilingual) unit, an English classroom, and a maths classroom. Further fieldwork took place at out-of-school events during Refugee Week and the West End Festival in Glasgow. The research spanned over 18 months and included 24 field visits.

In Phase 1 of the project the researcher was known to the management of both schools, which made access easy. Negotiating access to the pupils and learning spaces was particularly challenging during Phase 2, however, as the new researcher was unknown. Following a change in school management in the intervening period, staff were reluctant to have a researcher in their classroom, and building trust and relationships with the teachers and pupil participants was an ongoing process throughout Phase 2. Everyone who participated was given information about the research and all provided their informed consent.

Findings

Phase 1: primary and secondary 2003–05

Although EAL services had existed in Scotland for many years, this period of enhanced provision created opportunities to develop coherent Scottish policy for the education of bilingual learners. Bilingual pupils in Scotland are defined as those who use two or more languages in their daily lives (SEALCC, 2005). The policy documents *Learning in 2+ Languages (ibid.)* and *Languages for Life* (LTS, 2006) were produced during this period and were explicitly supportive of an additive bilingualism – viewed by Cummins (2000: 45) as one of the key indicators of a transformative/intercultural orientation to education.

Just as the Glasgow Asylum Seeker Support Project (see page 112) was a multi-agency response to demographic change, coinciding with this period was a proliferation of community projects that aimed to foster social cohesion. Such arts, culture, and sports projects were often based in the enabled cross-fertilization of cultural capital between the long-term inhabitants of these deprived areas and the newcomers who could be viewed as having few, if any, human capital resources. These efforts led in turn to the development of bonding social capital and, to a certain extent, bridging social capital (Coleman, 1988) but this is not to suggest that there were no tensions, as running alongside the educational and community investment was the pejorative portrayal of asylum-seekers in the media, and of immigration in general. See, for example, the use of the emotive terms 'bogus asylum-seekers' and 'bogus refugees' in a *Daily Mail* article (2006). Such language use had been fuelled by remarks made by Labour's Home Secretary David Blunkett, in a BBC radio programme on 24 April 2002. He asserted that children of asylum-seekers were *swamping British schools* and should be taught in immigration centres.

It was within this context that Phase 1 of the research was conducted by Geri Smyth (2006a and b). This research aimed to investigate the creative ways in which teachers were responding to a new demographic and the creativity employed by pupils as they attempted to adapt to a new school culture and a new language environment.

The context of teaching in Scotland was defined by curriculum guidelines (SOED, 1993), which were seen as placing content knowledge at the centre of education. Performativity was the goal, as Scotland was not considered to be scoring well on the international literacy and numeracy standards measured by PISA (Programme for International Student Assessment), PIRLS (Progress in International Reading Literacy Study), and TIMMS (Trends in International Mathematics and Science Study).

Teachers' agency was constrained by a highly structured curriculum and regular testing. The impact that these had on pupils whose first language was not the language of the classroom has been discussed by Smyth (2004). Given this context, in Phase 1 teachers felt liberated by the new arrivals. As these pupils could not be expected to compete in monolingual, monocultural assessments, teachers had to find new ways of working – and were thus given an opportunity to regain the professional capital that they had lost with the introduction of curriculum guidelines for children aged 5 to 14. The teachers in Phase 1 identified how the curriculum and assessment arrangements caused the pupils difficulty, instead of trying to legitimize their failure on grounds of their language difference or limited educational experience. In doing so, the teachers aligned themselves with Cummins's (2000) model of a transformative/intercultural orientation to education.

> I realized that in many cases they [the children] knew more than I did and I wanted to find out what they knew. I was able to throw the curriculum out of the window as I sought to provide the best education possible.
>
> (Primary teacher, 4 June 2004)

Having specialist EAL teachers – funded by the National Asylum Support Service (see page 112) – and understanding the interdependence of languages (Cummins, 1979) ensured that collaborative and co-constructed practice was focused on additive bilingualism. This enabled newly arrived pupils from asylum-seeking families also to have agency in the school system, as they brought their language and life experiences into the classroom.

> A linguistically mixed group of 10-year-old pupils were constructing a group poem, trying to imagine what they would see, hear, taste, smell, and touch in space. Ivan, recently arrived from Russia, told the group, 'You know the first man in space was from Russia like me.' This sparked considerable interest from the rest of the group and resulted in Ivan writing Yuri Gagarin's name in Russian into the poem and then teaching the rest of the group how to write their names in Russian. The resultant group poem was then signed by all four pupils in Russian characters, in homage to Gagarin.
>
> (Field notes from primary, 2 September 2003)

The teacher and pupil agency consequently established led to school practices that Smyth (2006a) likens to a multilingual conference. Teachers recognized that pupils had knowledge, skills, and linguistic capital that they did not share. They acknowledged the power of collaborative meaning-making and strived to offer opportunities for pupils to develop their meaning and understanding together. If teachers were the keynote speakers in this conference, the pupils acted as the skilled multilingual translators who had the greater shared audience awareness. Pupils were in many cases empowered by the pedagogy to take over the stage themselves.

Thus 12-year-old Carina from the Democratic Republic of Congo, having just written her first story in English and shared it with the younger children, was overheard telling the story in two other languages besides English, whereas the teacher facilitators could only have done so in English. When the researcher asked which language she had chosen to tell the story to a child who had first arrived at the school that day and why, Carina responded: 'I told her the story in French because she doesn't know English yet.' Her recognition that a child's 'not knowing' English is only temporary reflected her own linguistic development. In response to her telling the story in Lingala to a child who had been in the country longer than she herself had, she said: 'I did Lingala because it's her best language.'

In a very short time this pupil was able to utilize her linguistic capital and make decisions about which was the most appropriate language to use for different children. She could justify her choice on pedagogic grounds enabled as she was by the pedagogic orientation of the school and the teachers. In both the primary and secondary settings the pupils used creative learning strategies to overcome linguistic barriers. As the teachers strove to make the learning relevant, so the pupils increased their control and ownership of the learning and produced innovative outputs – evidencing the hallmarks of Jeffrey and Woods's (2009) creative learning.

During this period of ethnographic research the researcher spent time in the school staff rooms, where conversations were frequently concerned with what life was like for these children who had fled their country of origin and found themselves in Scotland's previously monolingual schools. Compared to the school, the external structures of society were not as inclusive and many families lived in constant fear that their claim for asylum would be rejected. One pupil told me on a daily basis, 'Tell them I'm a good girl' – 'them' being the powers who would decide whether her family would stay or be deported.

Teachers could come into work on one day and find that children who had been in their classroom the day before were no longer there; they were most likely detained by the UK Border Agency. So teachers had to utilize their professional capital to engage politically with the life issues of their pupils – one result of which was the development of the Glasgow Girls campaign group in Stringchurch Secondary School in 2004. This group of seven female pupils took their campaign to both the Scottish and the UK parliaments, fighting against the detention and deportation of their fellow pupils whose families' claims for asylum in the UK had been rejected. Their political activism was supported by the school's teachers, who helped them understand the opportunities for democratic expression in the UK. The group went on to win the Scottish Campaign of the Year Award in 2005 and their trophy was proudly displayed in the school foyer. This real and immediate citizenship education went beyond the confines of a syllabus, empowering the young people to take action and giving them knowledge and understanding of the workings of political systems and media. There were structural limitations to this citizenship, however, as those who have not yet been granted leave to remain in the UK cannot become UK citizens and do not, for example, have the right to vote and thus influence future policy.

The pupils from asylum-seeking families were all highly motivated to learn and *be* learners. Many of them had been denied education in their country of origin and they and their families saw education as the key to security and a better future. Very quickly the achievement levels at the secondary school – as measured by national examination results – improved dramatically, and the headteacher went on record as saying that this was down to the positive educational orientation of the young asylum-seekers.

Phase 2: secondary 2007–09

Between phases 1 and 2 of the project, we as researchers experienced institution and management change following the departure of the secondary school headteacher, a period of several months without a headteacher, and an eventual new management structure. In addition, the school's demographic had shifted once again. The majority of asylum-seeking families were granted leave to remain, and this saw them move from council housing into other areas of Glasgow. However, most children in their final years decided to remain at the secondary school and utilize the support of its EAL unit. During an interview the teachers described how the change in pupil demographic had a significant impact on the school's culture. They found that, because it was the bilingual children who had a positive impact on the attitudes towards learning and school, once their number declined the positive impact did so too.

Although the school building was modern and bright inside, teachers and pupils said that they disliked its boxy and 'call centre-like' architecture and that they missed the swimming pool and big theatre stage of the old building. It became clear to us that new does not invariably mean better – an impression that coalesced with the participants' opinion. Furthermore, ownership of space was not a given in the research site, as participants did not feel that the building provided what they wished for:

> The buildings they tore down were 50s and 60s buildings that had big drama stages, pits, backstage music things, swimming pool – then we could not find the money to support them ... and then we get this cheap and nasty building that is only good for a call centre.
>
> (Secondary teacher interview, 19 May 2009)

The implementation of another new curriculum – the Curriculum for Excellence (LTS, 2009) – also fell within Phase 2 of the project. Faced with its demands and the insecurities it aroused, as well as their concerns about the new management team, teachers were both reluctant to participate in the research and to provide information about their teaching experiences. They felt that the burden of bureaucracy had increased and that it stood in the way of their teaching. Teacher agency was reduced in the context of increased performativity, as this teacher's reference to the league table – that is, the published accounts of pupil performance – testifies:

> We, as teachers, are under so much pressure to get into [the] league table. We are stressed out having to attend to so much political stuff that we cannot do what easily could be done given the freedom, the time and the finances. People might say I am cynical, but it is cheaper to have aspects of society failing for the greater good.
>
> (Secondary school teacher interview, 19 May 2009)

Some of the children whose families were yet to be granted leave to remain were subject to detention. In the UK, if families that are refused leave to remain decide to ignore this decision, they may be forcibly removed from their homes and taken to detention centres pending deportation from the country. Right up until the final stages of Phase 2, children too were taken into detention centres – formerly prisons – where they were kept for an undetermined time – a practice that the Glasgow Girls campaigned against. After strong objection from the public and politicians, child detention was prohibited in Scotland – only for those families to be transported to detention centres in England.

When a child failed to arrive at school one morning, amid rumours of detention, staff and pupils alike were deeply affected. Our field notes from this period are full of the concerns, frustrations, and anger at these practices that the children expressed. The children that we spoke to were unsettled by the experience: some thought that their classmate had done something wrong and had been put into prison for criminal behaviour; those who had experienced displacement were left traumatized, worried that their classmate had been involved with the 'bad people' – meaning traffickers; other children who did not comprehend the situation regarded it as a form of adventure. Whatever the child's reaction, the impact of a schoolmate disappearing into detention reverberated among children and staff for weeks. This extract from our research field notes indicates that, although the school functions as a secure place for these young people, that cannot eradicate their daily fears:

> Because the class was so immersed in the topic of detention, trafficking, and immigration, the teacher came to me. She did not know if I knew about Kibby, and told me about the issue and also about Jake, who is missing for weeks now and is said to have been in hiding with his family. When Ms Lee told me Kibby's story,

she said 'concentration camp' instead of detention centre. She was utterly embarrassed by that slip-up but permitted me to use it, because for me it was significant, showing how deeply the incident affected the children as well as the teachers. The teacher had also told me that the children get worried when one of the asylum-seeker children was home sick; they instantaneously asked if the child got deported. It seemed to be a big issue for the children.

(Field notes, secondary school, 4 March 2008)

The issue of detention demonstrated that Mr Gee, the remaining EAL teacher at Stringchurch Secondary School, was indeed 'more than a teacher'. He lobbied with immigration lawyers, members of the Scottish Parliament, and non-governmental organizations to get families out of detention and children back into school. His particular understanding of the teacher role contributed to good practice in the EAL unit. The teachers in the EAL unit used creative teaching to give bilingual pupils meaningful learning experiences, placing great emphasis on peer support in learning and ownership of the learning process. Utilizing a variety of media – from books and international news websites to drawing – to support communication, the learning environment within the EAL unit was learner-centred and fostered the development of social capital – both among the pupils and between the teacher and the pupils.

The good practice evident in the EAL unit could benefit the school as a whole. While Mr Gee undertook occasional outreach work in mainstream classrooms, the good teaching practice within the EAL unit became isolated in Phase 2 of our project. This is not to say that other classrooms in the school are without good practice; the English classroom, for instance, presented strong possibilities for creative learning in this project. However, there was no underlying system to foster this approach to learning and teaching in the school.

Barriers and bridges

In both phases 1 and 2 of the project it was clear that the management orientation to teaching and learning had a profound effect on their success. Where the orientation allowed for teacher creativity, as in Phase 1, learners themselves were enabled to be creative and to utilize their linguistic and cultural capital in new environments. This requires a management position that goes beyond the external audit demands of a performative system. This, in turn, requires that management staff feel confident that their professional capital is sustainable within the system, that the knowledge and orientations that they learned from their initial engagement with the linguistically and culturally diverse pupils will be recognized and valued by the wider education system.

The successes of the newly arrived bilingual pupils need to be celebrated and news of them disseminated widely to ensure that macro-level demands of assessment and evaluation do not overtake the best practice opportunities, such as were demonstrated in Phase 1 and in the EAL unit in microcosm in Phase 2 in terms of creative pedagogies and social capital development. The impact of media discourse on vulnerable children cannot be overestimated, as it is difficult to sustain creative and positive approaches to learning when newspapers are printing daily stories that refer to you, your family, and your community as 'bogus' and 'illegal' and as 'swamping schools'. Therefore campaigns such as Oxfam's *Positive Images* are hugely important for schools to work alongside and spread good news about multilingualism in schools.

As stated at the begining of this chapter, Scotland has control of its own education system but immigration and asylum policy is determined by the UK government. This situation could lead to teachers in Scotland ignoring national legislation, but this was clearly not the case in either Phase 1 or Phase 2. Teacher involvement in meaningful and immediate citizenship education led to considerable empowerment of the pupils, further increased by the additive bilingualism practices adopted in the primary school.

This additive approach was enabled by educational policy at both Scottish and Glasgow City Council levels. In documenting the pedagogical approaches to be taken with bilingual learners, LTS (2006) urges teachers to maximize opportunities for use and development of home languages within the school. This is not always supported in practice and a strong multilingual institutional identity, as in Lady Jane Grey Primary School, needs to be fostered for the full benefits of this to be seen.

Cross-national implications for good practice

While the research reported in this chapter is by its nature local, there are certainly cross-national implications for the good practice discussed. The dynamics of change that led to these schools altering their institutional habitus are clearly not a Scottish-only phenomenon, as migration for political and economic reasons is on the increase globally. The ways in which schools respond to these changes and reform their identity informs the transition of community identity and fosters a genuine two-way integration. What was crucial for success in these two schools that we studied was first that both their teachers and their pupils were educated in critical literacy to enable their resistance to negative forces, and secondly that the schools did not operate in isolation but with full and meaningful community engagement.

Notes

[1] In Bourdieu's work, capital is recognized as having more than its traditional economic significance. Cultural capital refers to assets – such as competencies, skills, and qualifications – that enable holders to mobilize cultural authority. Social capital accrues to an individual or a group by virtue of their possessing a durable network of relationships of mutual acquaintance and recognition. On arrival in Scotland the refugee pupils possessed very limited cultural or social capital.

Habitus refers to the lifestyle, values, dispositions, and expectation of particular social groups that are acquired through the activities and experiences of everyday life. In this study we considered the habitus of the refugee pupils and of the teachers.

The field is the setting in which agents (teachers and pupils) are located, in this case the school. The position of each particular agent in the field is a result of interaction between the specific rules of the field, the habitus, the agent, and the agent's capital (Bourdieu and Wacquant, 1992).

References

Ball, S.J. (2000) 'Performativities and fabrications in the education economy: Towards the performative society?' *Australian Educational Researcher*, 27 (2), 1–23.

Bourdieu, P. (1977a) 'The economics of linguistic exchanges' [Electronic Version]. *Social Science Information* 16 (6), 645–68.

— (1997b) 'The forms of capital'. In Halsey, A.H., Launder, H., Brown, P., and Stuart Wells, A. (eds) *Education, Culture, Economy and Society*. Oxford: Oxford University Press.

Bourdieu, P. and Wacquant, L.J.D. (1992) *An Invitation to Reflexive Sociology*. Chicago and London: University of Chicago Press.

Bucholtz, M. and Hall, K. (2004). 'Language and identity'. In Duranti, A. (ed.) *A Companion to Linguistic Anthropology*. Oxford: Blackwell.

Claxton, G. (2006) 'Thinking at the edge: Developing soft creativity'. *Cambridge Journal of Education*, 36 (3), 351–62.

Coleman, J. (1988) 'Social capital in the creation of human capital'. *American Journal of Sociology*, 94 (suppl.), 95–120.

Csikszentmihalyi, M. (1997) *Creativity: Flow and the psychology of discovery and invention*. New York: Harper Perennial.

Cummins, J. (1979) 'Linguistic interdependence and the educational development of bilingual children'. *Review of Educational Research*, 49 (2), 222–51.

— (2000) *Language, Power and Pedagogy: Bilingual children in the crossfire*. Clevedon: Multilingual Matters.

— (2001) *Negotiating Identities: Education for empowerment in a diverse society*. Los Angeles: California Association for Bilingual Education.

Daily Mail (2006) 'Up to 80,000 bogus asylum-seekers granted amnesty'. Online. www.dailymail.co.uk/news/article-404269/Up-80-000-bogus-asylum-seekers-granted-amnesty.html#ixzz1r3WCkzDy (accessed March 2012).

Facer, K. and Williamson, B. (2002) *Designing Technologies to Support Creativity and Collaboration*. Bristol: Futurelab. Online. http://archive.futurelab.org.uk/resources/publications-reports-articles/handbooks/Handbook195 (accessed 21 August 2013).

Gardner, H. (1993) *Frames of Mind: The theory of multiple intelligences.* NewYork: Basic Books.

Gauntlett, D. (2007) *Creative Explorations: New approaches to identities and audiences.* London: Routledge.

Hall, S. (1993) 'The question of cultural identity'. In Hall, S., Held, D., and McGrew, T. (eds) *Modernity and its Futures.* Cambridge: Polity Press in association with the Open University.

Immigration and Asylum Act 1999 (c.33). London: HMSO.

Jeffrey, B. (2002) 'Performativity and primary teacher relations'. *Journal of Educational Policy,* 17 (5), 531–46.

— (2006) 'Creative teaching and learning: Towards a common discourse and practice' [Electronic Version]. *Cambridge Journal of Education,* 36 (3), 399–414.

Jeffrey, B. and Woods, P. (2009) *Creative Learning in the Primary School.* London: Routledge.

Keupp, H., Ahbe, T., Gmür, W., Höfer, R., Mitzscherlich, B., and Kraus, W. (2006) *Identitätskonstruktionen: Das Patchwork der Identitäten in der Spätmoderne.* 3rd ed. Reinbek bei Hamburg: Rowohlt.

Learning Teaching Scotland (2006) *Languages for Life Across the 3–18 Curriculum.* Glasgow: Learning Teaching Scotland.

— (2009) 'Curriculum for excellence'. Online. www.ltscotland.org.uk/images/all_experiences_outcomes_tcm4-539562.pdf (accessed June 2012).

Lewis, M. (2006) *Warm Welcome? Understanding public attitudes to asylum-seekers in Scotland.* London: Institute for Public Policy Research.

National Advisory Committee on Creative and Cultural Education (1999) *All Our Futures: Creativity, culture and education.* Online. www.cypni.org.uk/downloads/alloutfutures.pdf (accessed March 2012).

Oxfam, 'Positive Images'. Online. www.oxfam.org.uk/resources/ukpoverty/downloads/asylum_media_scotland.pdf (accessed May 2012).

Reay, D. (1998) '"Always knowing" and "never being sure": Institutional and familial habituses and higher education choice'. *Journal of Education Policy,* 13 (4), 519–29.

Scottish English as an Additional Language Co-ordinators' Council (2005) *Learning in 2+Languages.* Glasgow: Learning and Teaching Scotland.

Scottish Government, The (2007) 'One Scotland Many Cultures'. Online. www.scotland.gov.uk/News/Releases/2007/01/26113250 (accessed May 2012).

— (2008) *Tackling Scotland's gang culture.* Press release of 14 April 2008. Online www.scotland.gov.uk/News/Releases/2008/04/14095308 (accessed March 2012).

— (2009) *Scottish Index of Multiple Deprivation (SIMD): 2009 General Report.* Edinburgh: National Statistics.

— (2011a) 'Pupils – Independent schools'. Online. www.scotland.gov.uk/Topics/Statistics/Browse/School-Education/TrendIndSchools (accessed May 2012).

— (2011b) 'Pupil census, Supplementary data 2011'. Online. www.scotland.gov.uk/Topics/Statistics/Browse/School-Education/supppupils2011 (accessed May 2012).

Scottish Office Education Department (1993) *The Structure and Balance of the Curriculum 5–14.* Edinburgh.

Smyth, G. (2004) 'Down the plughole: Pitfalls of testing the writing of L2 pupils'. In Couzijn, M., Rijlaarsdam, G., and Van den Bergh, H. (eds) *Effective Teaching of Learning and Writing.* Amsterdam: Kluwer.

— (2006a) 'Bilingual pupil's creative responses to a monolingual curriculum'. In Jeffrey, B. (ed) *Creative Learning Practices: European experiences*. London: Tuffnell Press.

— (2006b) 'Multilingual conferencing: Effective teaching of children from refugee and asylum seeking families'. *Improving Schools*, 9 (2,) 99–109.

— (2010) 'Bilingual teachers: What role do they actually play in education?' In Ringen, B.-K. and Kjorven, O.K. (eds) *Teacher Diversity in a Diverse School: Challenges and opportunities for teacher education*. Vallset: Opplandske Bokforlag.

Smyth G., MacBride, G., Paton, G., and Sheridan, N. (2010) Social capital and refugee children: does it help their integration and education in Scottish schools? *Journal of Childhood and Adolescence, special issue on Young Refugees* 5 (2).

Walford, G. (2008) 'The nature of educational ethnography'. In Walford, G. (ed) *How to do Educational Ethnography*. London: Tufnell Press.

Wren, K. (2004) *Building Bridges: Local responses to the resettlement of asylum-seekers in Glasgow*. Glasgow: Scottish Centre for Research on Social Justice with The Community Responses Co-ordinating Group and The European Refugee Fund.

Chapter 8

Social justice for English language learners at Parkdown Secondary School in Toronto

Antoinette Gagné and Stephanie Soto Gordon

Introduction

Our case study describes how a high school in Toronto with a diverse pupil population enacts the principles of social justice, equity, and inclusive education embedded in both national and provincial Canadian policies.

Social justice can be defined in a number of ways but the underlying principles of equity and inclusion remain:

- The social and economic resources of society are distributed for the benefit of all people (Schookner, 2002)
- A process is operating through which society attains a more equitable distribution of power in the political, economic, and social realms (Hunsaker and Hanzl, 2003)
- These principles are based upon the belief that each individual and group within a given society has a right to civil liberties, equal opportunity, fairness, and participation in the educational, economic, institutional, social, and moral freedoms and responsibilities valued by the community (Degan and Disman, 2003)

The Equity and Inclusive Education in Ontario Schools policy operationalizes social justice in the following ways:

> We envision an inclusive education system in Ontario in which all students, parents, and other members of the school community are welcomed and respected; every student is supported and inspired to succeed in a culture of high expectations for learning. To achieve an equitable and inclusive school climate, school boards

and schools will strive to ensure that all members of the school community feel safe, comfortable, and accepted. We want all staff and students to value diversity and to demonstrate respect for others and a commitment to establishing a just, caring society.

(Ontario Ministry of Education, 2009)

The Toronto District School Board (TDSB) Director, Chris Spence, has posted the following message on the board website: 'Hope is what drives improvement. And improving our schools and ultimately our students' outcomes is what we're all hoping – and striving – for' (2011a).

In this chapter we describe the context and two related conceptual frameworks pertaining to the structure and strategies necessary to ensure success for English language learners, and present the findings of research conducted over a five-year period at Parkdown, an inclusive secondary school with a diverse pupil population in Toronto, Canada. We discuss various facets of this school to demonstrate how social justice is enacted and how its diverse learners are empowered. The terms 'immigrant pupil' and 'English language learner' (ELL) are used interchangeably as the vast majority of pupils learning English as an additional language at Parkdown are also immigrants. In a few cases, we use the term 'pupils with limited proficiency in English' to identity a subset of learners who are at the early stages of learning English. Many of the pupils involved in our study, however, had already achieved a level of proficiency in English that allowed them to express complex ideas and function in mainstream classes. We use the terms 'Canadian-born pupils' and 'native speakers' interchangeably because, in most cases, Parkdown pupils born in Canada are native speakers of English.

Three contexts that frame this research are now highlighted: the City of Toronto, the Toronto District School Board, and the English as a Second Language (ESL) Program at Parkdown Secondary School.

The City of Toronto

According to Statistics Canada (2007), of the million-plus immigrants who arrived in Canada from 2001 to 2006, 52.3 per cent settled in Ontario. It is reported that 'one third are under the age of 19, and three-quarters are from countries where English is not the first language' (People for Education, 2008: 20). Of the immigrants who live in Ontario, 46 per cent chose Toronto as their place of residence in the period 2001–06 (Statistics Canada, 2007), making Toronto the world's second-most multicultural city after Miami (Wikimedia Foundation, 2006). The communities in Toronto represent most ethnic groups in the world. According to the 2006 census, in 2001 57.7 per cent of Torontonians spoke English as their mother tongue; by 2006, this number had fallen to 54.1 per cent (Statistics Canada, 2007).

The school board

The Toronto District School Board is the largest school board in Canada and one of the largest in North America. It includes 451 elementary schools with 181,000 pupils; 104 secondary schools with 89,000 pupils; and five adult schools with 14,000 pupils. Fifity-three per cent of these pupils do not have English as their first language. More than 80 languages are present in the schools and more than 30 per cent of all pupils were born outside of Canada, immigrants from a total of 175 countries. Furthermore, over 10 per cent of all pupils have been in Canada for three years or less. More specifically, Yau and O'Reilly (2007) report that 42 per cent of secondary school pupils in the district were born outside Canada. When considering racial background in secondary schools, the percentages are as follows: 33 per cent are white, 19 per cent are South Asian, 20 per cent are East Asian, 12 per cent are black, 5 per cent are of mixed race, 3 per cent are Southeast Asian, 2 per cent are Latin American, and 3 per cent are aboriginal.

Parkdown Secondary School

Parkdown is a semestered secondary school known for its strong academic programmes. It is particularly recognized for having the following special features: an Advanced Placement Programme for enriched studies for senior pupils in such areas as calculus, economics, computer studies, French, and English literature; a programme for gifted pupils that forms part of the Special Education Programme; a specialized programme in mathematics, computer technology, English, and science; and a wide variety of co-curricular activities including athletics, the arts, robotics, cultural clubs, and pupil government. [para break]In 2011, the population of the school in was 1,107, 56 per cent being male. Of the pupil body, approximately 65 per cent speak English as an additional language and 20 per cent of these were born outside Canada and have been living in the country for less than five years; 9 per cent have been in Canada for two years or less; and 11 per cent have been in Canada for 3 to 4 years. According to the document Enrolment-Listing of Student Demographics (Toronto District School Board, 2009a), 25 per cent of the recent arrivals speak Russian, 14 per cent Tagalog, 8 per cent Hebrew or Korean, 5 per cent Chinese or Spanish, and 3 per cent Turkish; the remainder of the English language learners speak various other languages. A document referring to the mother tongues spoken at the school indicates that 33 per cent of the pupil population speak English as a first language, 14 per cent speak Russian as a first language, 12 per cent speak Chinese and Korean as first languages, and 5 per cent Tagalog. The rest of the population is very diverse and, therefore, speak various languages as their first language (Toronto District School Board, 2009b).

The teaching staff includes 29 men and 43 women, and 14 of them are immigrants to Canada. The racial, religious, ethnic, and linguistic backgrounds of the teachers, as described in their own words, include: two black, 22 of mainly English or French-European heritage, one Central American, five Chinese, one Egyptian, two Greek, one Indian, one Iranian, four Italian, one Japanese, 14 Jewish, one Muslim, one Philipino, one Polish, three Romanian, two Russian, and one Spanish.

Conceptual frameworks

Two interrelated conceptual frameworks serve as lenses through which to view the data gathered at Parkdown Secondary School over the five years from 2006 to 2011.

Thomas and Collier's Prism Model

Thomas and Collier (1999) conducted a longitudinal study of the records of over 700,000 linguistic minority pupils in five US school boards between 1982 and 1996. Their goal was to determine which pupil, programme, and instructional variables have the greatest impact on the long-term academic achievement of ELLs. Their findings have provided schools with instructional recommendations for effective programming for immigrant pupils and ELLs, and offered policymakers guidance to support language-learners' long-term academic success.

Collier and Thomas (2009) and Thomas and Collier (2002) found that most ELLs achieved academic success in English when their schools strove to: implement cognitively complex, grade-level academic instruction in the pupils' first language for part of the school day and in English for the rest of the day; use current approaches to teaching the academic curriculum, such as cooperative learning strategies and thematic units in the pupils' first language and in English; and create a socioculturally supportive environment for learning in two languages. A conceptual framework known as the Prism Model (Thomas and Collier, 1997) also emerged from the research. It consists of four components or processes – sociocultural, linguistic, academic, and cognitive – which the authors describe as 'driving' language acquisition and academic learning in schools. Since each component is interdependent, a comprehensive educational programme for language learners requires all of them to be in place.

Sociocultural processes

The authors describe the sociocultural component as the heart of the Prism Model. It includes the social and cultural processes that occur in the everyday life of pupils and that extend to their past, present, and future experiences, their home, school, and community environments, and their broader societal interactions and experiences. It involves individual pupil variables such as self-esteem, motivation, anxiety, and other affective factors. For example, if a pupil feels isolated from the mainstream pupil population or experiences discrimination, this can impact how he or she responds to his or her educational environment. A socioculturally supportive environment values both the rich life experiences and multicultural or multilingual background that all pupils bring to the classroom (Collier and Thomas, 2007).

Language development

The language development component of the Prism Model includes all aspects of language development: such as phonology, vocabulary, morphology, syntax, semantics, pragmatics, and discourse. The authors insist that all pupils be given the opportunity to develop sufficient proficiency in their first language (L1) to manage cognitively demanding tasks. They assert that this knowledge of their L1 will allow ELLs to develop a level of proficiency in English similar to that of their peers for whom English is a first language. Thomas and Collier (2002) found that the development of the pupils' L1 is an essential factor in their second-language (L2) development and overall educational attainment. Pupils who have the opportunity to do academic work in their L1 have greater long-term academic success in their L2.

Academic development

Thomas and Collier (2002) suggest that school programmes that postpone or interrupt academic development by focusing solely on developing proficiency in English and waiting to incorporate academic development until pupils attain a certain level in their L2 are detrimental to the overall achievement of ELLs. Collier and Thomas (2009) recommend that ELLs complete a certain amount of academically demanding work in their LI and that ESL teachers integrate meaningful academic content into their ESL lessons. Furthermore, they explain that, through academic work in both their L1 and L2, ELLs develop a broader vocabulary, master the subtleties of the sociolinguistic and discourse dimensions of language, and reach higher levels of cognitive development.

Cognitive development

The final component of the Prism Model is cognitive development: the natural, subconscious process that occurs developmentally from birth, through formal schooling and beyond. Cognitive development involves the construction of thought processes such as remembering, problem-solving, and decision-making. Young children generally develop thought processes through interactions in their L1. The authors suggest that teachers can build on this knowledge base, as it is an important foundation for further cognitive development in both the L1 and L2. Thomas and Collier (2002) summarize multiple studies that provide evidence that children who reach a stage of full cognitive development in two languages enjoy cognitive advantages over monolinguals.

Freeman and Freeman's Keys to Academic Success

By focusing on specific strategies to support pupils at classroom level, the classroom-based research that Freeman, Mercuri, and Freeman (2001) carried out with teachers of ELLs extends the Prism Model. The authors (ibid. and Freeman and Freeman, 2007) identified four key components of an educational programme for ELLs, which they deem essential to the latter's long-term academic achievement, their acquisition of English, and their overall feelings of belonging within the school environment.

Freeman, Mercuri, and Freeman (ibid.) refer to the four components or teaching strategies to help ELLs succeed academically as the 'Four Keys to Academic Success'. The first key involves engaging pupils in a challenging, theme-based curriculum to develop academic concepts. In thematic units, different areas of the curriculum can be interrelated and vocabulary is repeated naturally in different contexts. When the curriculum is organized around a theme, thematic units provide pupils with opportunities to transfer the knowledge and skills they learn in one subject to another (ibid.).

The second key encourages teachers to draw on pupils' backgrounds, including their experiences, cultures, and languages. By activating pupils' prior knowledge, teachers can make English input more comprehensible by allowing ELLs to build additional concepts and ideas onto a prior knowledge foundation.

The third key suggests that organizing collaborative activities and scaffolding instruction will help build pupils' proficiency in academic English. Freeman, Mercuri, and Freeman (ibid.) encourage teachers of ELLs to provide challenging and cognitively demanding lessons, and to include supports to ensure that the input is comprehensible. Scaffolding strategies include using temporary supports such as visuals, demonstrations, dramatization activities, acting out meaning, and explaining words and linguistic structures.

The fourth key encourages teachers to support the development of confident pupils who value school and value themselves as learners. Freeman, Mercuri, and Freemand (ibid.) encourage teachers to recognize each pupil's intellectual and personal talents and to affirm their cultural, linguistic, and personal identities, as this creates the conditions by which the pupils invest their entire identity in the learning process.

Research methodology

Our case study introduces findings from research conducted over a five-year period at Parkdown Secondary School. Our research was conducted in four stages of study over this period, with the findings of new stage building on those of the previous one. Although our focus has generally been on the pupils, the four studies that feed into this case also involved formal and informal interviews with teachers and pupils, surveys for teachers and pupils, and classroom-level and school-level observation as well as document analysis.

The overall purpose of each study was to enhance our understanding of how to create a more inclusive environment where both immigrant pupils and Canadian-born pupils can thrive.

Findings

The ESL programme at Parkdown Secondary School

Although expanding course selections for ELLs was one of the goals of its school plan, Parkdown Secondary School still struggles to provide a full range of ESL and sheltered subject courses to meet the needs of ELLs with varying levels of proficiency in English (Soto Gordon, 2010). As well as providing access to mainstream, grade-level content and support for the development of English language proficiency, sheltered subject courses offer meaningful instruction in content areas like social studies and science. Moreover, an average 30 to 40 ELLs register for these courses once the school year is in progress, but these additional pupils are not always taken into consideration when determining course offerings.

When guidance counsellors create a school timetable for immigrant pupils who are learning English in the autumn and winter semester, these pupils are typically placed in an ESL class appropriate to their language ability level. ELLs are also typically enrolled in multilevel subject courses for students with ESL as well as being integrated in other classes with native English-speakers. The multilevel sheltered subject courses for pupils with ESL include civics/careers, computer and information science, drama, French, geography, history, introduction to anthropology, psychology and sociology, learning strategies, mathematics, and science. When there is an insufficient number of ELLs to warrant offering these subject courses, ELLs are integrated into regular classes where there is far less support for them as they attempt to develop their proficiency in English. In any case, as pupils with ESL improve their level of English proficiency, they spend more and more time in mainstream classes.

Furthermore, when pupils are in ESL level 1 or ESL level 2, guidance counsellors avoid placing them in subject-specific classes like geography, history, introduction to anthropology, psychology, and sociology as these require a significant amount of written work. We observed, however, that the breadth of courses offered to accommodate the needs of ELLs was directly related to enrolment figures. There are often problems with timetabling – especially for pupils with limited proficiency in English such as those registered in ESL level 1 or level 2. It is not uncommon for these pupils to be enrolled in classes for which their level of proficiency in English does not equip them. This highlights the requirement for additional sheltered subject courses that are appropriate for immigrant pupils with limited proficiency in English – not an easy task, considering the frequent funding cuts at the school board (Toronto District School Board, 2012).

The co-curricular activities specific to ESL pupils are the ESL Ambassadors Club and the ESL Drama Club. By 2011, the ESL Ambassadors Club had been in place for seven years and welcomes new pupils to the school by pairing them with a pupil who shares their first language. The ESL Drama Club had been in place for five years and its members were actively involved in the research for this case study. Other clubs in which pupils with ESL may participate include cultural clubs such as the Russian, Korean, Jewish, and Hispanic clubs. They also often participate in an evening event that celebrates multiculturalism with ethnic crafts, food, and entertainment.

Pupil life at Parkdown

In addition to the clubs that ELLs tend to favour, Parkdown offers a large selection of clubs including those with the following foci: the environment, chess, anime, pupil partnerships, the school newspaper and website, the school yearbook, model United Nations, gay/straight alliance, global development, fundraising, science, academic competitions, creative writing, and computer programming.

There are also numerous culture clubs, associations, and alliances, which have the following foci: African-Caribbean culture, Chinese culture, Christian fellowship, Culturama, Filipino culture, Jewish culture, Korean culture, Muslim Pupils Association, South Asian Alliance, Chinese Culture Club.

To provide a sense of what is involved, here are some descriptions of the clubs from the school website:

- Chinese Culture Club is where all those who are interested and enjoy learning about Chinese culture assemble! We frequently play Chinese related activities and watch dramas and movies. Not only do we bond as a Chinese community, but as a multicultural one, with our various members of different backgrounds. Yellow Power Unite!
- South Asian Alliance is where Parkdown pupils can come together to acknowledge and celebrate South Asian culture. During club meetings pupils can discuss various issues regarding the South Asian community and learn more about South Asian traditions and culture. The South Asian Alliance also organises and participates in school events such as Culturama and Parktoberfest to raise awareness of South Asian culture at our school!
- Muslim Students Association seeks to serve the needs of Muslim pupils at Parkdown through holding regular Friday prayers, giving presentations, fundraising and much more!
- African Caribbean Culture Club is a social organisation made up of members from Parkdown's ethnically diverse school community. Pupils meet weekly to discuss hot topics that affect the Black community, as well as to watch movies and TV shows that have a focus on Black culture. The club also strives to increase the awareness of the Afro-Caribbean presence in the school through various cultural events.
- Culturama was started almost ten years ago. Culturama is an annual performance at Parkdown Secondary School organised by the members of the club. On the night of Culturama, pupils perform songs, dances, martial arts, etc, coupled with a wide selection of food and drinks from various cultures.

The range of clubs available depends on the composition of the pupil population each year. However, with such a rich variety of clubs, Parkdown is a school where almost every pupil can find an appropriate club. We observed that pupils' decisions about which club to become a member of were based on which teacher was overseeing it. For many ELLs, the safety of knowing the teacher sponsoring the club was more important than its actual focus.

Other opportunities for learning

The music programme includes a concert band and choir, jazz band and choir, junior wind ensemble, and guitars. Sports teams include badminton, baseball, basketball, volleyball, cross-country running, floor hockey, golf, ice hockey, rugby, soccer, softball, tennis, track and field, ultimate frisbee, and wrestling. Field trips include visits to art galleries, theatres, hospitals, the Ontario Science Centre and Royal Ontario Museum, and rock climbing, horseback riding, and beach volleyball. French-language pupils also visit Quebec, arts pupils visit New York, and social science pupils travel to Europe.

While pupils had access to a great variety of clubs, we found that many immigrant pupils were unable to participate when the clubs were held after school. Several of these pupils have after-school jobs or are expected to contribute to the running of the household by taking care of younger siblings and so on.

Pupil success initiative

As part of a broader pupil success initiative launched across Ontario, Parkdown has a pupil success room where pupils can receive support. The intention is to allow them to 'rescue' or 'recover' a credited course if they are at risk of failing or leaving school without the requirements for high school graduation. Pupils with special needs or learning difficulties receive support and can take courses focused on learning strategies in the resource room as well. The centre also monitors the progress of those ELLs who are new to Canada, who are offered a full complement of ESL courses. The guidance counsellors work with ELLs and can connect them to peer tutors or a tutoring group where necessary. The guidance staff also works with the Ambassadors' Club to ensure that each new pupil is paired with a peer who speaks the same language.

Parent engagement

To reach out to as many parents as possible, Parkdown has developed several strategies to communicate with families. These include six report cards, automated voice recordings, a frequently updated school website, a biannual newsletter, parent/teacher interviews, and several information evenings, as well as special event evenings. Parkdown's school council meets every month and has parent representation to ensure that information regarding educational opportunities and policies makes its way to all families. School council meetings also ensure that parents have the opportunity to communicate with the administration directly.

As many parents and caregivers do not speak English, newsletters and messages are translated if requested, and interpreters are made available for meetings with teachers and other school staff such as guidance counsellors. A number of settlement workers from different backgrounds are present at school events to ensure that immigrant parents are actively involved. While there are many opportunities for parents and caregivers to participate at school, most are prevented from doing so because of the demands of their jobs, household responsibilities, limited proficiency in English, and a general lack of familiarity with the Canadian school system, and an attendant feeling of discomfort.

Community engagement

Parkdown works closely with the Toronto Police Service and a school-specific safety hotline is available to the school community. Parkdown has also established innovative and meaningful partnerships with the local shopping mall, community health outreach centre, and residence for seniors. In addition, Parkdown pupils fundraise persistently on behalf of various charitable organizations, while pupils enrolled in co-op courses (apprenticeships) are placed in community businesses to complete their fieldwork. These various partnerships focus on the needs of pupils as well as the community, and therefore serve both well.

School improvement plan overview

Parkdown's school improvement plan is directly connected to the three priorities underpinning the Toronto District School Board's (2011b) Our Vision of Hope: pupil achievement, parent and community engagement and financial stability. The board stipulates that every decision made in its schools must support a system where the first priority is to support learning for all. On its website, the board indicates that: 'The Toronto District School Board is united in support of every pupil. The collective efforts must ensure that each pupil is able to achieve or exceed the standards set out in our four system goals.'

To establish a school improvement plan, the school community evaluates the results of province-wide assessment measures in literacy and numeracy every year, as well as numerous other indicators of school success. Some of the strategies put in place to ensure that all Parkdown pupils develop a high level of literacy and numeracy are now described.

Literacy

As Parkdown has many immigrant pupils who find the province-wide literacy test challenging, after-school literacy support has been made available. All pupils take an evaluated mock literacy test and receive formative feedback on their performance. In addition, reading and writing activities similar to those appearing on the literacy test are integrated in Grade 9 and Grade 10 English courses and resources are provided to pupils who want to practise their reading and writing outside of the classroom. In Grade 9 and Grade 10 English courses, emphasis is placed on reading and writing strategies. Parkdown has also made cross-curricular literacy a priority, such that all Grade 9 and Grade 10 courses include subject-specific reading and writing activities to give pupils further opportunities to develop their literacy skills.

Numeracy

Cross-curricular numeracy is also a priority at Parkdown, where all subject courses integrate activities to give pupils further opportunities to develop their numeracy skills. Pupils are prepared for the province-wide mathemathics test with practice questions and a mock test. Peer tutoring, 'extra help' tuition, and multiple contests offer pupils both remediation and enrichment opportunities. Technology – e.g. SmartBoards, clickers, and graphing calculators – is integrated into lessons and pupils acquire the necessary skills to apply the mathematical knowledge needed to solve problems effectively.

Pathways

To support the province-wide Pathways initiative, pupils in all grades are given a range of opportunities to explore career possibilities. Grade 9 pupils can participate in a programme that allows them to spend a day with a family memberat his or her place of work, and they are also invited to visit the school's Career Centre. In their career studies classes, Grade 10 pupils are introduced to the Who Am I? Programme and My Blue Print to support their post-secondary exploration.

In Grade 11 and Grade 12 pupils can gain work experience if they enrol in a co-op course. Opportunities to take Career Interest Inventories, combined with visits from college and university representatives and parent information evenings, give pupils further chances to explore post-secondary-school options. Course selection week and numerous post-secondary mentorship opportunities help pupils to make informed decisions about their future endeavours.

Social justice at Parkdown

While the provision of numerous opportunities for all pupils – in class and beyond – ensures that social justice is operationalized at Parkdown, an informal survey completed in theautumn of 2008 showed that ELLS do encounter barriers to their participation in mainstream classes and school activities. In addition, our study revealed a disconnection between immigrant pupils learning English as an additional language and Canadian-born pupils: the extent to which thesegroups were mutually integrated was limited. As part of our ongoing research at Parkdown, we invited ten pupils from each group to work together for a year in an attempt to get to know each other better. We asked them to produce a series of recommendations that could create a more inclusive and equitable culture while pupils worked towards increased integration.

Barriers to interaction

Barriers to interaction in the classroom and the school between English language learners and their native-speaking peers were revealed by the data. Both groups agreed that language acted as a barrier. ELLs and Canadian-born pupils who were also native speakers of English (NSs) saw ELLs' lack of proficiency in English as an obstacle: 'I was afraid to make gramma[tical] mistakes, I couldn't talk and I felt very isolated.'Conversely, NSs spoke of their ELL peers' use of another language in class or school as another significant barrier:

> The two girls took charge, and when we tried to put in our ideas they wouldn't listen to us and they would speak in a different language and act as though they were talking down to us because we couldn't understand what they were saying. That was one issue in that group.

The need to complete tasks or assignments in groups or play on a sports team made up of both ELLs and NSs proved challenging for both groups:

> I didn't have a group, so I asked the teacher to put me in a group and he did. I could tell, though, that the group didn't really want me to be there because they thought I wasn't going to contribute ... it made me feel really lonely and shy, and that made it even worse to be by myself.

Feelings of exclusion were experienced by both groups and this was identified as an important barrier to their mutual interaction: 'I felt like a ghost, because I was there but nobody saw me. No one actually cared.' 'Sometimes, the ELLs will group together and start talking in their native tongue. I realize that it is just easier for them to communicate that way, but I can't help but feel a bit left out ....' Lastly, the group of ELLs cited their initial lack of familiarity with the school's culture as another aspect that hindered interaction with their peers: 'Everything from the hallways to the teachers looked very different to me.'

Self-help strategies

Both ELLs and NSs indicated that they could help themselves in the classroom by engaging other people when they encountered challenges. NSs said they should take the initiative to engage peers and be more accepting and inclusive in their interactions with ELLs. A few ELLs and NSs indicated that anticipating challenges as well as looking for alternative means of communication, such as athletic activities, might empower pupils to overcome barriers. Table 8.1 provides a summary of the self-help strategies suggested by participants at different stages during the project.

Table 8.1: Summary of suggested self-help strategies

Overcoming Barriers: Perspectives of ELLs on self-help strategies to interact with NSs	Overcoming Barriers: Perspectives of NSs on self-help strategies to interact with ELLs
Classroom • work harder • imagine presentations are with only ELLs; this alleviates fear • communicate with NSs in order to find a shared goal • imagine there is no language difference **School** • be less shy • attempt conversation with NSs • approach NSs with a group of ELL friends • social networking via email is less intimidating than speaking face to face • be positive • imagine that all people are the same	**Classroom** • tap into strengths of group members – imagining connections with work • request accommodations • ask the opinions of others • envision ways to help increase ELLs' confidence through conversation – outside group-work time to help create an inclusive environment **School** • approach someone one-to-one or with only a few people, rather than in a group of people • imagine how the ELL might feel • recall past experiences that are similar to the experiences of ELLs

Suggested strategies for peers

ELLs indicated that NSs could help by engaging them when they were faced with barriers. Likewise, NSs called on ELLs to be tolerant and to engage them when they met difficulties. NSs emphasised that they wanted ELLs to reach out to them.

Table 8.2: Summary of suggested strategies for peers

Overcoming Barriers: Perspectives of ELLs	Overcoming Barriers: Perspectives of NSs
Support from NSs ELLs stated that NSs could help them with the challenges they faced. Suggestions for their peers included: **Classroom** • trust ELLs with the work • empower ELLs to lead the group • treat ELLs like NSs – give the ELLs freedom to work independently then edit work with them • reach out to ELLs to be in their group • be direct with ELLs about the need to correct work – 'don't do it behind their back' • ask ELLs for their opinion **School** • invite ELLs to participate in a team • reach out to ELLs to include them in a group • greet ELLs in the hallways/ be friendly • have food parties • have a club with ELLs and NSs as ambassadors	**Support from ELLs** NSs suggested that ELLs could help build bridges with NSs. The proposed strategies included: **Classroom** • show enthusiasm towards school work • be open about academic ability; this builds trust **School** • introduce other ELLs to NSs • use a safe, one-on-one basis to communicate

Suggested strategies for educators and parents

ELLs indicated that teachers could offer support by engaging pupils and by adopting inclusive processes for forming groups. In the school community, ELLs stated that both parents and teachers could help them face challenges by being reassuring. As with the classroom, NSs called on parents and teachers to promote acceptance and inclusion of all pupils to reduce barriers between ELLs and NSs in the school community. Interestingly, both groups believed that teachers should act as a bridge between the ELLs and NSs.

Table 8.3: Summary of suggested strategies for educators and parents

Overcoming Barriers: Perspectives of ELLs	Overcoming Barriers: Perspectives of NSs

Support from educators
 	
ELLs believe that teachers can help them overcome the challenges they face when interacting with NSs. They suggest the following strategies:
 	
Classroom
 	
• provide accommodations
  ○ extra time may help NSs empower the ELLs – time pressure is removed
  ○ discussions in small groups instead of in front of the whole class
• adopt inclusive processes for grouping pupils
  ○ place people who don't know each other in groups
  ○ do not force pupils to pick groups
  ○ include both ELLs and NSs in groups
  ○ check in with ELLs – one-to-one time
	Support from educators
	
	NSs point out that teachers could support both ELLs and NSs in their interactions with each other. They suggest the following strategies:
	
	Classroom
	
	• provide accommodations for ELLs
	• group work
	  ○ make groups that prevent the exclusion of ELLs
	  ○ design groups based on pupil strengths
	  ○ assign daily logs describing participation to give pupils feedback on their progress
	
	School
	
	• reassure ELLs through conversation – one-to-one attention

School

- keep class quiet during morning announcements so that everyone can hear about co-curricular activities
- be welcoming by approaching ELLs to offer support for co-curricular involvement
- greet pupils in the hallways
- show kind body language – eye contact/less formal
- provide avenues for ELLs to mix with NSs, such as this project
- stress the importance of multiculturalism
- promote school-wide projects

- encourage the sharing of food from different parts of the world
- introduce ELLs to reliable, kind NS pupils
- understand the connection between what goes on in the classroom and the school more broadly

Support from parents	**Support from educators and administrators**
ELLs offer a few suggestions so that their parents can support them in their integration in the classroom and school community:	NSs strongly recommend that educators adopt the following strategies to nurture the relationship between ELLs and NSs:
Classroom	**Classroom**
• check in with ELLs about their classroom experiences – one-to-one time • communicate with teachers	• have specialized programmes for ELLs within the regular classroom • provide accommodations so the grades of ELLs reflect their abilities and not their language skills • ensure that NSs are reminded about communication and inclusiveness
School	
• encourage ELLs to meet other people outside their cultural group • remind ELLs of family goals • encourage children to reconnect with their interests in the new country	

	School • introduce ELLs to NSs – build connections • identify NSs who have empathy with immigrants • monitor relationships • encourage discussion on inclusion

Revisiting the conceptual frameworks

Thomas and Collier's Prism Model

In reviewing the data, it becomes clear that Parkdown has operationalized many aspects of Thomas and Collier's Prism Model (1997) to ensure the success of English language learners. We found that, for the most part, cognitively complex, grade-level academic instruction in English was provided in ESL classes, sheltered ESL subject classes, and mainstream courses. Our findings also revealed that current approaches to teaching the academic curriculum, such as cooperative learning strategies and thematic units, were used across grades and in many courses. We also saw a great deal of evidence that a socioculturally supportive environment existed for English learners via the provision of a wide range of cultural and religious clubs, extra-curricular activities, and additional supports beyond the classroom.

Although Thomas and Collier call for instruction in immigrant pupils' L1 for part of the day, this was not possible at Parkdown due to the large number of first languages spoken by the pupils. However, a range of initiatives and services – including the ESL Ambassadors Club, the availability of interpreters and settlement workers, multilingual messages for families, and a celebration of multiculturalism through Culturama – demonstrate that pupils' first language and cultural background are valued.

Freeman, Mercuri, and Freeman's Fourth Key to Academic Success

Freeman, Mercuri, and Freeman's (2001) and Freeman and Freeman's (2007) first three keys to academic success for ELLs are similar to Thomas and Collier's Prism Model (see page 134–5). Consequently we focus on the fourth key, which relates directly to the research work presented on the integration of immigrant pupils and Canadian-born pupils.

The work of the ESL drama teacher, who also ran Parkdown's ESL Drama Club, provides an example of how the fourth key was operationalized with pupils. This teacher reached out to the Canadian-born pupils, inviting them to join members of the ESL Drama Club to explore their sense of belonging, share their experiences, and talk about the barriers they faced in relating to each other in the classroom and in the school. Over time, they formed a community with a common purpose: of creating a DVD in which they would share their experiences, self-help strategies, and suggestions for peer, teacher, and parent support. Seeing the project develop from idea to product gave these pupils a sense of what is possible, and helped them to feel confident about their ability to interact with each other and to contribute to Canadian society in important ways. Table 8.4 presents a few quotes from ELLs and NSs about how participating in this project affected them.

Table 8.4: Perspectives on participation in the project.

English Language Learners	Canadian-born Native Speakers of English
I felt and thought differently about native pupils, because when you get to know a person beyond 'hi' and 'bye', suddenly all the anti, judgemental thoughts are going away. We had different activities with the native-speakers that encouraged me to learn about Canadian culture. This process gave me more confidence to get involved and meet new and other people. It showed me that it is possible to get out from the 'ESL bubble'... This experience helped me to understand that native speakers are willing to be friends with newcomers. Before, I was afraid of starting a conversation with other pupils other than ESL pupils, but now, I am not afraid to express myself.	Overall, I have felt a lot more comfortable approaching English language learners and having a conversation with them. It was a good experience to have to meet new people and talk to them about anything. It taught me that we are all very similar as well as unique. I've really earned an understanding as to why English language learners appear to be defensive when I first meet them. I have many English language learners that I am good friends with. At the beginning though, I thought most of them were just not talkative and were ignorant by nature. I never knew that for some it is a very big difference coming to a new country.

Conclusion

Although Parkdown Secondary School offers a number of programmes geared toward the success of ELLs, as well as enrichment opportunities through clubs, extra-curricular activities, and family and community outreach initiatives, additional professional development opportunities related to the integration of immigrant pupils must be made available to teachers and school administrators. Both ELLs and Canadian-born pupils spoke about the need for increased school-level communication and outreach strategies to ensure that they are given the tools to come together in the classroom and beyond, and fully experience social justice at school.

References

Collier, V.P. and Thomas, W.P. (2007) 'Predicting second language academic success in English using the Prism Model'. In Cummins, J. and Davison, C. (eds), *International Handbook of English Language Teaching*, Part 1. New York: Springer.

—(2009) *Educating English Learners for a Transformed World*. Albuquerque, NM: Fuente Press.

Degan, R. and Disman, M. (2003) *Cultural Competency Handbook*. Toronto: University of Toronto, Department of Public Health Sciences.

Freeman, D. and Freeman, Y. (2007) *English Language Learners: The essential guide*. New York: Scholastic.

Freeman, Y., Mercuri, S., and Freeman, D. (2001) 'Keys to success for bilingual students with limited formal schooling'. *Bilingual Research Journal*, 25 (1 and 2), 203–13.

Hunsaker, J. and Hanzl, B. (2003) *Understanding Social Justice Philanthropy*. Washington DC: National Committee for Responsive Philanthropy.

Ontario Ministry of Education (2009) *Equity and Inclusive Education in Ontario Schools Guidelines for Policy Development and Implementation*. Toronto.

People for Education (2008) 'Annual Report on Ontario's Public Schools'. Online. www.peopleforeducation.com/reportonschools08 (accessed 3 May 2009).

Schookner, M. (2002) *An Inclusion Lens: Workbook for looking at social and economic exclusion and inclusion*. Public Health Agency of Canada, Population and Public Health Branch Atlantic Canada.

Soto Gordon, S. (2010) 'A case study on multi-level language ability groupings in an ESL secondary school classroom: Are we making the right choices?' Unpublished PhD thesis, University of Toronto.

Statistics Canada (2007) 'Census trends for Census subdivisions – 2006 Census'. Statistics Canada Catalogue no. 92-596-XWE. Ottawa. Online. www12.statcan. ca/english/census06/data/trends/Index.cfm (accessed 8 May 2009).

Thomas, W.P. and Collier, V.P. (1997) 'Two languages are better than one'. *Educational Leadership*, 55 (4), 23–6.

— (1999) 'Accelerated schooling for English language learners'. *Educational Leadership*, 56 (7), 46–9.

— (2002) *A National Study of School Effectiveness for Language Minority Students' Long-term Academic Achievement*. Santa Cruz, CA: Center for Research on Education, Diversity and Excellence, University of California atSanta Cruz.

Toronto Disctrict School Board (2009a) 'Facts and figures'. Online. www.tdsb.on.ca/communications/tdsbfacts.html (accessed 10 May 2009).

— (2009b) 'Mother Tongues'. Online. www.tdsb.on.ca/about_us/media_room/room. asp?show=allNews&view=detailed&self=17969 (accessed 11 May 2009).

— (2011a) 'Chris's Page'. Online. www.tdsb.on.ca/_site/ViewItem.asp?siteid=10391 &menuid=22244&pageid=19358 (accessed 12 December 2011).

— (2011b) 'Our Vision of Hope'. Online. www.tdsb.on.ca/_site/ViewItem.asp?siteid =10496&menuid=27835&pageid=23941 (accessed 12 December 2011).

— (2012) 'TDSB funding needs not a crisis, but a crunch'. Online. www.tdsb.on.ca/ wwwdocuments/Trustees/Ward_11/docs/Budget per cent202012 per cent20Ward per cent20Slide per cent20Presentation per cent201-2-12.pdf (accessed 12 February 2012).

Wikimedia Foundation (2006) 'Demographics of Toronto'. Online. http:// en.wikipedia.org/wiki/Demographics_of_Toronto (accessed 11 December 2011).

Yau, M. and O'Reilly, J. (2007) *2006 Student Census, Grades 7–12: System overview* (Board Report No 07/08-01). Toronto: Toronto District School Board.

Index